M000113806

ENDORSEMENTS

I don't know another person who studies as much to help other people maximize their potential as Dave. Here he has compiled important gems of wisdom and insight from many sources that would take most people years to compile on their own and has put it in this brief, hard-hitting, and unique read that can be absorbed in just a few hours and that I'm sure will help many.

—RICK JOYNER
Founder and Executive Director
of MorningStar Ministries

In *Ignite Your Passion, Chart Your Course, Own Your Life*, Dave Yarnes provides something we all yearn for and desperately need—perspective. His insights are rocks to stand on, and from those vantage points we can survey life and chart our course. Reading this concise book is a great investment of time and energy.

—ROBERT WHITLOW
best-selling author of *A Time to Stand*

If you have any desire to grow in depth and power personally, professionally, and spiritually, *Ignite Your Passion, Chart Your Course, Own Your Life* is your guide. I know Dave Yarnes personally, and he is a remarkable entrepreneur and Christian leader who has established a profound blend of passionate spirituality and excellent business acumen. He brings a fresh perspective on how to live a full life and build the foundations for lasting prosperity.

—MIKE BICKLE
International House of Prayer of Kansas City

Dave Yarnes' book is a wisdom-filled combination of spiritual and practical steps to make our careers fulfilling. We take Scripture at its word that God desires prosperity for His children. The question is how to then achieve that prosperity. Dave, with some 30 years of successful business to his credit, gives us a guide of how to do it. Characteristically, his *Ignite Your Passion, Chart Your Course, Own Your Life* begins with the Circle of Spirit. The Circle of Skill and the Circle of Self-Mastery follow. I highly recommend this book to those who wish to reach prosperity and do it God's way. From my 40 years of experience, I know that any time I followed the principles Dave outlines, I was successful. And any time I did not, my efforts led to failure. Now I know why.

—NICHOLAS F. S. PAPANICOLAOU
former majority shareholder and chairman of
Aston Martin Lagonda Group, UK

I highly recommend Dave Yarnes' new book, *Ignite Your Passion, Chart Your Course, Own Your Life*. I have known Dave for more than 20 years and have traveled and ministered with him on three continents. The field-tested insights on leadership unveiled in this book will change your life. Dave's chapter on the Circle of Self-Mastery is worth the price of the entire book. Thank you, Dave, for writing this much-needed book for the present and future generations of leadership.

—LARRY KREIDER
director of DOVE International

Rarely do I pick up a book these days that can hold me to the end without a break. But Dr. Dave Yarnes' *Ignite Your Passion, Chart Your Course, Own Your Life* is an exception to that rule.

With magnetic page-turning power, Dr. Yarnes packs tons of compelling wisdom within a powerful little book, written in an easy-to-follow writing style, that can change lives, if only the reader will heed its wisdom. The "Three Circle Strategy" of spirit, skill, and self-mastery is both revolutionary in thought and simplistically brilliant at the same time. It's as if the practical secrets to success in life have been there all along but made invisible by the thick fog of life's many distractions. The "Three Circle Strategy" is a bright sunbeam that removes the fog hiding those secrets.

Put another way, in a manner that is easy to digest and to grasp, Dr. Yarnes reveals the unique keys to personal success that have been there all along but yet are so hard to see because of the mundane clutter of life's distractions.

I predict that *Ignite Your Passion, Chart Your Course, Own Your Life* will become one of those power-packed "little books" that never leave your bedside, much like Napoleon Hill's classic *Think and Grow Rich* and Og Mandino's *The Greatest Salesman in the World*. The practical nuggets of truth for success and self-mastery within the three circles will become fountains of motivation and encouragement that will last a lifetime.

In the area of self-help, *Ignite Your Passion, Chart Your Course, Own Your Life* is destined to become a classic. I can't wait to give a copy to my son and am honored to wholeheartedly endorse it.

—DON BROWN
author of the *Publishers Weekly* national bestseller
The Last Fighter Pilot, the Amazon national bestsellers
Treason and *The Malacca Conspiracy, Call Sign Extortion
17*, and Zondervan's Navy Justice Series

David Yarnes has a unique ability to approach any field and succeed by discovering the essential success formula hidden in it. What's great about Dave is that he does not teach others until he has mastered the craft himself. He has done this in more than one field—from mixed martial arts, to banking, to managing award-winning hotels, and now to mentoring organizations and leaders. He brings his unique gifts to us again in his most recent book, *Ignite Your Passion, Chart Your Course, Own Your Life*, which is loaded with insights that can make the difference between mediocrity and mastery. I encourage you to buy this for yourself and for two or three friends. Tell them you would like to follow up with them and see what you all gleaned. You will be amazed at what you'll discover.

—Dr. Lance Wallnau
founder of Lance Learning Group, Dallas, Texas

It is with true joy and excitement I write this endorsement of Dave Yarnes' new book, *Ignite Your Passion, Chart Your Course, Own Your Life*. I've known Dave for several years and ministered with him on numerous occasions. Dave is remarkably gifted and anointed to help others advance in their journey to the next level of success. Dave's Kingdom Business Association conferences stress character and integrity along with strategy and encouragement to follow your God given dreams. You will receive insights and understanding and become better equipped to navigate life's pathway by the content of these pages.

—Bobby Conner
Founder of Eagles View Ministries

IGNITE
YOUR PASSION
CHART
YOUR COURSE
OWN
YOUR LIFE

DAVE YARNES

IGNITE
YOUR PASSION
CHART
YOUR COURSE
OWN
YOUR LIFE

THE 3 CIRCLE STRATEGY
FOR A FULFILLING LIFE

DESTINY IMAGE® PUBLISHERS, INC.
P.O. Box 310, Shippensburg, PA 17257-0310
"Promoting Inspired Lives."

This book and all other Destiny Image and Destiny Image Fiction books are available at Christian bookstores and distributors worldwide.

Cover design by Christian Rafetto
Interior design by Terry Clifton
Edited by Sarah C. Godwin

For more information on foreign distributors, call 717-532-3040.

Reach us on the Internet: www.destinyimage.com.

ISBN 13 TP: 978-0-7684-1774-6
ISBN 13 eBook: 978-0-7684-1775-3
ISBN 13 HC: 978-0-7684-1777-7
ISBN 13 LP: 978-0-7684-1776-0

For Worldwide Distribution, Printed in the U.S.A.
1 2 3 4 5 6 7 8 / 22 21 20 19 18

DEDICATION

This book is dedicated to my three sons, Mathew, Nathan, and Sam. My hope is that you will be able to have the type of rich and fulfilling life I have enjoyed. I feel like your childhood was one big experiment. We've had some great adventures together; now go and make your own. With great love and admiration, I remain your biggest fan.

ACKNOWLEDGMENTS

Thanks to my wife Gina for putting up with the chaos my adventurous spirit often brought into our lives. I want to thank and acknowledge all those who have given me support and encouragement throughout this process. Especially I want to thank Sarah from Sarah C. Godwin Editing who has been a constant source of expertise and encouragement. Thanks to all those business professionals and entrepreneurs who I have met through my role as the founder of the Kingdom Business Association and the National Federation of Christian Businesses. You are the ones who have committed yourselves to personal excellence and continual self-improvement. I also want to thank those who want their job to have greater impact than just providing a paycheck—those who strive for mastery in all areas of life and want their impact to be far-reaching and long lasting. You continue to inspire me.

CONTENTS

INTRODUCTION

Almost 20 years ago, I started teaching a seminar series which became the source for much of the research and material for this book. Simultaneously, I was building a career as an entrepreneur. Over the past two decades, I have developed an award-winning hotel, a New York based hedge fund, a performing arts theater, a pharmaceutical company, a national bank, and other enterprises. Each one helped develop the lessons that played an important role in the "fleshing out" of the principles you're about to discover.

Along with my own personal experiences, and perhaps more importantly, I have been able to interview hundreds of individuals who have been impacted by these lessons and learn what elements have had the most sustained positive outcome. With each interview, I discovered some of the training material I thought was important didn't receive the reaction and application I had expected, so I eliminated or modified that material. Other material seemed to have a profound impact on many individuals from differing audiences, so I expanded and developed it in more detail. The lessons I learned while developing and refining the content have been invaluable. I and others have been able to improve this material and its presentation to make it more and more effective and easier to apply.

The core message has been refined into three overarching master topics to create the Three Circle Strategy. It has taken considerable time and effort to keep the core message simple, easy to understand, and easy to apply.

BEFORE YOU BEGIN, DOWNLOAD THE FREE *3C COMPANION GUIDE*

Ignite Your Passion, Chart Your Course, Own Your Life has lessons that you're about to learn that have helped many and are easily applied to your life on a daily basis. For years, participants using this material requested a journal or workbook they could use to personalize their responses and create their own plan and application of the material. Our response was to create the *3C Companion Guide*. The *3C Companion Guide* is a free essential companion resource that is easily downloaded and is both printable (if you're like me and still like paper and pen) or usable in e-format. The *3C Companion Guide* has expanded material for each section and contains corresponding questions which will walk you through simple, practical application steps. Each section of this workbook is designed to give you space to reflect. All this is designed to help you integrate the material effectively into your personal plan. You can download your free copy of the *3C Companion Guide* at www.DaveYarnes.com. By answering the 3C Exercises at the end of each chapter and engaging with the free *3C Companion Guide,* you will be able to capture the practical application side of this material.

PRINCIPLES, NOT METHODS

Have you observed how many people have a desire to change but don't have a plan? Developing and maintaining a plan for a fulfilling and prosperous future can be one of the most richly rewarding activities in life. It can also require some deep reflection and self-analysis. I will show you how to create your own life plan based on the 3C Strategy for fulfilment and prosperity.

Principles are universal truths and they are transferable. Methods, specific tactics, and procedures are often difficult to transfer from person to person. Principles can be applied regardless of your age, background, or current level of success. Your plan must be customized to fit you. You will find that this single difference of applying true principles will become an important key to unlocking your potential and sustaining a more abundant life.

When you create the right plan to fulfill your dream and then you work to take care of it, it can grow and produce fruit you may never have imagined. No one intentionally plants weeds in a garden, but if you plant a garden and do nothing to care for it on a regular basis, weeds will grow. The same is true about your life plan. Sustainability, fulfillment, and true prosperity take some effort, but yield results that last.

What I write about here, I honestly strive to intentionally practice and live. Most of the significant positive changes in my life have come from understanding and applying the principles that lie ahead in these chapters. I hope your experience is as life changing as mine.

CHAPTER 1

YOUR PURPOSE, YOUR PASSION, YOUR PATH

"Do not go where the path may
lead, go instead where there is
no path and leave a trail."
—RALPH WALDO EMERSON

Phil was on his way back from a time management and personal planning seminar. This one was costly, $1,500 for the entrance fee and sacrificing three days, his entire long weekend, when there were many things that needed tending to around the house. His young son and daughter were home with a sitter while his wife worked for the weekend. Phil had been doing well as a senior manager in a local wealth management firm. To others, he appeared to have it all together. He was always an example of hard work, seemed to be well organized, and was a good family man. But inside, Phil felt like he was living someone else's life. He didn't want to be ungrateful for all he had, but there were a lot of sacrifices along the way, and he just felt like there was something more that he was called to be. Now approaching his late 30s, if there was a time to make a change, this was the time.

Coming back from the seminar had given him more ideas and energy than ever before, but still there was an elusive thought. In the back of his mind, he felt like he had the tools to move forward but didn't have clarity on what that future looked like. And he was desperate to put it into focus.

Mary's story was a little bit different. She felt like she had really landed a great job, good career path, and rare employment opportunity seven months ago with an up-and-coming graphic arts and marketing firm. She liked the neighborhood where the office was located so much that she got an apartment two blocks away from her office in a trendy eclectic part of town. Her work was interesting and fulfilling. Then last month, the senior partner came in and told her that they were downsizing and closing the office. They were generous with her severance package, since she had just moved and was banking on this job. She estimated she had about three months of living expenses, after cutting back in every area she could, before she had to be settled into a new job.

She was just finishing up a weeklong career development seminar that was part of her severance package. Most of the information was interesting, but the topics were mostly things she already knew—résumé building, job searching, developing interview skills. These were things she felt very confident about; however, there was one session that stirred her more deeply than the others. A local restaurant owner came in and shared his experience of starting his first restaurant. He shared stories of the sacrifice and commitment that were necessary, especially in the early years. There was one thing he said that stuck in the back of her mind, and she couldn't get it out. He said, "I ultimately would have failed if I didn't have a passion for what I do and an ability to see the finished product." That thought haunted her. What was her passion? What was that *thing* that she would sacrifice for? Was she being too idealistic to even have those thoughts? Shouldn't she just be concerned about getting a job, saving up for a starter home, and meeting the man of her dreams?

Bob and Sue had just flown back from Michigan where they finally sold the home they had lived in for the past 25 years. It was bittersweet. They knew their time there was over. The kids were grown, had lives of their own, and had scattered across the country. Now Bob and Sue finally had a chance to enjoy their retirement condo in Florida. After all, wasn't this what they had been planning for?

They were six months into their retirement, both of them felt fit and healthy in their late 60s.

But more and more, day by day, they had begun to experience a sinking feeling that they had made a mistake somewhere. There were no surprises or real pain points in their newly found retirement life. Their new community was as expected—pleasant and quiet.

They had planned well financially, which allowed them to eat out a couple nights a week and maintain a membership at the local golf course / country club. But night after night, as they ate dinner together, they wondered if they had made the right decision, or had they just bought into a plan that wasn't truly theirs.

For almost 20 years, I have heard and analyzed hundreds of stories like these. The individuals have different names, different details, and various locations and circumstances, but they all follow seemingly scripted patterns. My interest and focus on creating and refining life strategies started in my late 20s, as I began to have more employees and did some counseling at the church I attended. I have always been a "people person" and have tried personally and professionally to lend a hand and some sound advice where I could. My study grew from a casual interest to a deep desire for understanding and competency. Some stories were difficult to hear, and I often felt grossly ill-equipped to give advice.

What started as a small leisurely pursuit became a core of my life study. From undergraduate and doctoral degree to my business and pastoral career, there has been a common question: how can I help people live a fulfilling life?

THE TWO APPROACHES TO LIFE PLANNING

On the last day of a sold-out conference I was hosting, a young lady named Karen came to me and said something that completely changed my perspective on the topic of life planning. The conference was designed for business owners who were attempting to break through to a new level of success. I had co-hosted 15 events like this, which had all sold out, and the feedback on the long-term effectiveness was astonishing. The conference was wrapping up; it was the early afternoon of the last day of the weekend event. I was feeling confident, validated, and quite proud of all we had accomplished together.

Karen approached me as I was drinking a cup of coffee on the back deck of the mountain lodge where our event was being held. I was watching the last of the low-lying mist disappear from the valley when Karen asked if she could chat with me. She was in her mid-30s and had already grown two impressive consumer electronics companies. And now, after having sold one of them, she was looking for direction for the next season of her life.

"I wanted to thank you for an amazing weekend," she started off. "Everything... the material, the food, the venue, has been first class," she continued, and then there was a long pause, which I knew meant there was a deeper question or concern.

"Karen, feel free to say what's on your mind," I said. "You may have a question that others are considering as well, and I appreciate any feedback you can give us."

"I have read a lot of your material, and this is the second conference I have attended, but I think there is something wrong with me.

I'm just not able to get it like everyone else. I have some type of blockage or maybe it's something I just can't figure out."

She was visually shaken, so I asked her to sit and reassured her for a while, but as she began to articulate her perceived conflict, I realized she was not the one with the problem. I was the one with the problem. Or more clearly, there was a major hole in what I had been teaching, and Karen fell right into it. I have spent years trying to understand the problem that Karen unfolded that day. From there, as I looked back through conference surveys and emails from readers, I realized she wasn't alone. Many had tried to express similar thoughts.

Until the conversation with Karen, my approach to life planning had a singular path. This was the same path that many of those I work with had promoted as well. As I re-examined material from other popular authors and presenters on the topics of life planning and personal coaching, I saw similar gaps, holes, and deficiencies in their material.

My approach, which had helped so many, had a common theme that follows a familiar script. First, begin to understand yourself and your environment, then gain clarity on the goals of the life plan you are seeking to accomplish. The more clarity you can get on your future direction and "future self," the better. Equally important is to align your passion with your newly defined direction. The more clarity you can achieve and the more it aligns with your passion, the more you will be able to generate the thrust to attain a fulfilling future.

Let me state clearly that I still absolutely believe this to be true. I will continue to write about and present this information. But Karen helped me to realize that this was not the singular answer for all individuals in all walks of life. If this was my only approach, I would be doing a great disservice to many people.

On that day, Karen said, "I have never had complete clarity before starting any of my ventures. I have gone through all the exercises and spent a considerable time in prayer, but I have never gotten high-level clarity or high-level focused passion about any of my past successful pursuits."

Karen was successful and living a rich and fulfilling life, but because I and others had been so singular in our approach to life planning, she felt she was somehow not measuring up.

Many people can gain high-level clarity about the precise nature and composition of their future, and they can couple this with high-level passion, using the tools and techniques in the material that I and others have promoted. For others, clarity is elusive. The picture and definition of their future seems shrouded. I have come to discover that this lack of clarity occurs almost as frequently as the high-level clarity individuals.

I feel the material ahead is equally applicable to both types of people—those with extreme clarity about their future and those who have a desire for transition, but only have a general feel for what their future entails. Neither group is wrong, and they are equally common. These two perspectives can often occur in the same individual at different seasons of life.

For one group of individuals, let's call these the "*Clarions*," they will use the material ahead to achieve high-level clarity and high-level passion for their fulfilling life. Using the practical tactics and resources from the material ahead, they will create a plan that leads to their fulfilling future. They will use the material in the *3C Companion Guide* to chart their course.

The second group of individuals, let's call these the *"Voyagers,"* will have equally fulfilling rewarding lives, but find their direction much differently. While *Clarions* have a very specific, definable destination in mind, *Voyagers* have more of a general compass heading. Think of it like this, the *Clarions* are able to get an exact destination and plug it into their internal GPS system. Although they may get rerouted from time to time, due to traffic accidents or detours, their destination remains constant. In contrast, *Voyagers* have a general sense of heading or purpose, but no real clear idea of the destination.

Voyagers know instinctively that where they are right now is not their final destination, and they have a general idea of how they should be moving forward, but their approach to life planning will be completely different than the *Clarions*. If their life-planning approach does not take this into account, they can often have the same experience as Karen. They can feel everyone else "gets it" but they do not. This can lead to frustration, a self-defeating mindset, and often inactivity toward any goals.

Most of the life and career-development material that I've researched works well for *Clarions*, but it needs significant adjustments for those in the *Voyager* category. Even if you are a consummate *Clarion*, there can be *Voyager* seasons in life. While at one point in time you may have a crystal-clear objective and aligning passion for your life, there may be other areas of your life that may be vague, and you only have a general directional heading. *Voyagers*, or maybe those of us in a *Voyager* season, can miss out on opportunities to develop and refine our life plans if we wait for *Clarion* vision and strategies.

If we don't give room for this distinction and understanding, we will have major issues in our life plan. If you are a *Voyager*, or simply an individual in a *Voyager* state of life, and you encounter material that continuously directs you to get more and more clarity, this can result in frustration and despair. It could also lead to something even more dangerous; it could stall your initiative or keep you from seeing a way to move forward. It's simply not how you are internally "wired."

Again both *Clarions* and *Voyagers* are valid and can achieve equal levels of a fulfilling, rewarding, and enriching life; however, the approaches will be vastly different.

I knew a man who, as a young boy, was fascinated with the insect world. His life revolved around catching, quantifying, and identifying every creeping, crawling thing he could find. In high school, he was drawn to biology and science. In college, he knew that he wanted to study various species of insects and their effect on crops and our environment. He only focused on applying to universities with noted programs in these specific areas.

> Again both *Clarions* and *Voyagers* are valid and can achieve equal levels of a fulfilling, rewarding, and enriching life

Today, he is one of the most successful, well-researched, and well-published authors on the subject of certain types of insects. He is fulfilled and enriched as he engages in his dream job on a daily basis. He is an extreme example of a *Clarion*. His approach is significant to understand. First, his life goals were aligned with his passion; we will talk about how important this is in later chapters. Secondly, he began to narrowly define the objectives of his fulfilling life. Third, he concentrated his efforts and his resources to get the training and education and to position himself for the opportunities that would propel him, thrust him, into that place of his most fulfilling life.

On the other side of the spectrum, there is a friend of mine who is a great statesman who has represented some of the world's most influential leaders. He has been behind the scenes, participating in some of the most critical global events of our time. He told me that nothing he has done of extreme significance came from a clear, pre-defined plan. He simply had a general direction and a vague feeling of the destination he was looking for. He coupled this with having the faith and perception to take opportunities as they presented themselves that seemed to align with his general sense of purpose and direction. He would find himself in circumstances where he would have a busy week planned and an opportunity to travel to a distant country would present itself out of the blue. Somehow, he knew to put other things aside and capitalize on this opportunity. These seemingly arbitrary circumstances led him to some of his most fulfilling and enriching achievements. He is a highly effective, fulfilled *Voyager*.

The material ahead is designed to help and profit both *Clarions* and *Voyagers*. I've also taken the time to include personal stories and reflections from my life which fall into both categories. The Three Circle Strategy chapters, the accompanying 3C Exercises at the end of each section, and the material in the *3C Companion Guide* will aid you, whether you're crystal clear and passionate about your future life or you're trying hard to define your path. In both instances, you'll find the material easy to understand and easy to apply.

CHAPTER 2

DISCOVER WHAT MATTERS MOST AND SET YOUR COURSE

"You're the only person with a Dream
quite like yours. And you have it for a
reason: to draw you toward the kind
of life you were born to love!"

—BRUCE WILKINSON, *The Dream Giver*[1]

A "CLARION" SEASON

As our small van bounced along the back roads of East Africa, my mind was clouded by sickness and malaria medication. Everything seemed to be moving in slow motion. It was increasingly difficult for me to stay focused.

I was spending a month overseas in remote areas of Kenya, Uganda, and Rwanda meeting with key African leaders. Our team was developing two micro communities that could house approximately 200 AIDS orphans and a childcare center in a large slum area. We were also helping establish a micro-lending program that would support small businesses in Africa.

The trip had been exhausting. My energy level was extremely low. Many of the sites we visited were accessible only by six- to eight-hour rides in vans or SUVs that went winding endlessly over dangerous roads. Along the way, we had witnessed many accidents. Even when we reached a destination, our accommodations were often nothing more than small upgraded mud huts with external pit latrines. Our hosts always gave us the best lodging and food they could provide, but much of it was very different from even the most meager standards in the developed world.

MET BY GUNS

Near the end of our journey, we approached a border crossing. As our van slowed at the border station, we suddenly realized that something was drastically wrong. Without warning, police and local militia crowded around our van at the makeshift checkpoint. People were shouting and waving guns. They surrounded us and forced us off the road.

Although I couldn't understand the language they were speaking, I knew immediately they were demanding that we exit the van. There was a strong possibility that our money, luggage, supplies, and camera equipment would be seized for inspection. Past experience told me we would have little hope of having anything returned.

As I slid open the van door, a local policeman pointed excitedly at me with his automatic rifle and shouted something unintelligible. I remember thinking that his violent actions and gestures might cause the weapon to fire accidentally.

As I emerged from the van, I was carrying a small paper folder in my hand. Our acting interpreter told me nervously that the policeman wanted me to set it down and leave it in the van for inspection.

Without hesitation, I said calmly but firmly, *"No—I refuse to do that."*

Startled, the policeman studied my face. This was not the response he expected to hear. For a moment, he became even more insistent that the folder be placed down, but I just looked back at him without moving. Seeing my resolve and looking again at the items, he allowed me to take the folder with me as I left my other belongings behind.

All of my other possessions—money, equipment, supplies, and even my reserve of cash and credit cards hidden in one of the bags which were all now left at the mercy of these officers—were of no consequence to me compared to the folder in my hand.

THE FOLDER

During that month in East Africa, as we had bounced along those back roads, I had gradually been transported in my mind and spirit away from all the discomforts and inconveniences of my surroundings into an unexpected place of incredible mental clarity. I could see clearly my dreams for the future, what mattered most to me, and what I wanted my life accomplishments to be. I could see clearly my own personal destiny and the people who I wanted to spend my life with. Not only did I have a clear vision of where I wanted to be, but I also had an understanding of the course my life needed to take in order to get there. I did not understand it at the time, but I was in a *Clarion* season, and I did not know how long it would last. I had to capture the clarity and seize this unusual opportunity.

During the long African nights, often by the light of a small lantern, I had begun to write down my goals, vision for the future, core purposes, and what I valued most. I had also listed people who I wanted to bring with me as I lived out my dream.

This supernatural ability to discover my dream and put it into writing was so powerful that no one—not even at gunpoint—was going to take my dream away from me.

Before I had left for Africa, I had been juggling unimaginable layers of priorities in both business and ministry. Sometimes I did not know where it would all lead. With the benefit of this new clarity I had gained on my journey, I had painstakingly written all of my newfound revelations in one document, describing my vision for my life. I had no backup copy. Even in my sickened and disoriented state at this border crossing, I had enough sense to clutch this document and hold onto it, despite the threats. I realized that everything but this was replaceable.

I entitled this document my "Personal Vision Newsletter" and I have had it with me, in one form or another, ever since that day. The pages ahead will provide the prompts for you to create a similar work I now call "the 3C Plan."

SETTING MY COURSE FROM A "CLARION" SEASON

When *Clarion* seasons come, do everything within your power to capture the direction and take action. Times of great clarity can afford laser-like plans and accompanying passion. The time spent in Africa developing clear and passionate goals and direction for my future was an unusual time of high-level clarity. It is now many years since that encounter in East Africa. My Personal Vision Newsletter

> When Clarion seasons come, do everything within your power to capture the direction and take action.

has been revised and rewritten hundreds of times. It has made the transition from one planner to the next—often tattered by the time it was transcribed again. My vision has even made the quantum leap to the paperless planning system that I now use.

From that day in Africa, my life changed as I captured direction and transformed it into an actionable plan. Ever since, I have set my course accordingly, navigating toward each objective, working backward from the end goal I visualized while on my Africa expedition in that *Clarion* season.

WISDOM OF LEADERS FOR "VOYAGER" SEASONS

I still remember his question as if it were yesterday. I was sitting in Washington Reagan Airport, completely engrossed in a conversation with a great spiritual leader, my friend James Cannon.

Commuters rushed by in all directions, but I remember being so focused that it seemed as if the noise and distractions around us were muted. His question was big, and I knew I had not considered it in the past. I also knew it would help set the course for the rest of my life.

James was well known for his incredible business and his philanthropic exploits. I was young, my companies growing and philanthropic efforts just beginning. Ever learning, I always looked forward to whatever time I could spend with him. I asked him about his success. I thought of as many questions I could throw at him on a number of topics.

Over the years, I have found ways to grab moments with key leaders wherever and whenever I can. If I know someone is traveling and has a long layover or is stopping at a certain airport, I often arrange my schedule to coincide with theirs, to grab a few minutes in their busy lives. I had to sacrifice and be intentional, but it was always worth it.

My topic for the day with James centered on some orphanages that he and I had financially underwritten in East Africa. The need was immense. The AIDS pandemic was ravaging villages and creating masses of orphans. We talked about lessons we had learned. We discussed watching the children grow up to lead fulfilling lives. We remarked, as we poured money into this devastating need, that our personal bank accounts grew somehow miraculously, supernaturally.

A question about personal focus had been forming in my mind. I said, "I feel so passionate about the work in Africa, but I am also seeing incredible opportunity in business here in the States. Plus, my family is young and the travel is often grueling. There are so many directions to consider. I just want to make sure I'm focusing my efforts wisely."

His look seemed to intensify and he stared at me for a moment. Then he looked at his watch and glanced at his ticket. He continued in a more serious tone, "I have to run, but there is something I have wanted to tell you that seems obvious to me but might not be to you."

THE QUESTION

"You are at a crossroads, and it seems as if you are trying to go in a lot of directions, but there is really one question to be asked, and you're the only one that can answer it. Once you do, you will be able to focus your energy on making it a reality. Then every other aspect will fall in place naturally. When all is said and done, what will you have considered a worthy life?"

With that, he picked up his bag, we said our goodbyes, and he walked off to his gate.

The question was so simple but haunting. Looking backward from the end of my days, what would I consider a worthy life? What would be my measure of fulfilment and prosperity?

This is an example of a *Voyager* season in my life. I desired change and had a deep sense that there were bigger things ahead for my life, but I didn't have concrete objectives or high-level clarity. So I adopted a *Voyager* strategy—move forward with a few directives to see how things looked once I made some general progress. The key to success with *Voyagers* is a bias toward movement and action. Don't just stay inactive, looking for complete clarity. Explore, move forward in the directions you have available, see how things develop. You may have to backtrack and retrace some steps and make adjustments, but this process helps eliminate some options and bring definition to others. I lacked the clarity at that moment to definitively answer Jim's

> The key to success with *Voyagers* is a bias toward movement and action.

question succinctly. What would I consider a worthy life? What would be my measure of fulfilment and prosperity? But I knew the answers would become clearer as I moved forward.

TAKING OWNERSHIP

The two stories above represent pivotal points in my life. One was a *Clarion* season the other a *Voyager*. Action is a key for both types of seasons. Research shows that there are two main ways individuals approach the topic of change and movement toward fulfilment and prosperity. There are those who believe they have no control over exterior conditions and are not able to influence or affect change. On the other end of the spectrum, there are those who believe they can change and control most aspects of their own environment. This second group has a strong understanding that they can dramatically influence their personal world through their actions.

The first group will be driven by circumstances and not by choices. The second group will live a more dynamic and forward-driven life.

The bottom line is the more influence you believe you have, the more things in your life you will try to influence and the more success you will sustain. Just trying to exert influence creates a higher probability of actually being able to make change.

As we get started in this life-changing material, take a moment to adjust your thoughts. Attitude makes the difference between those who live their dream, feel fulfilled, and create the type of life they believe they were destined for and those who live at the mercy of their current surroundings and circumstances. Before you move on, pause a moment to think deeply about your attitude, and make a commitment to yourself to approach this material with a fresh sense of empowerment.

CORE PASSION AND CHANGE

You may have tried to muster this passion from time to time as projects and platforms demand. But if you're like most people, when the moment passes or the project ends, the passion fades. Why? This type of passion is what I call "situational passion." It exists only in relation to a cause. However, when you undertake the task of uncovering and defining what matters most to you personally, a true, lasting type of passion and clarity is released. Let me say it simply, clarity and visualization of what matters most to you will create a lifestyle of passion. This is what I have come to label "core passion" and it is a powerful tool for continuous change.

When you undertake the task of uncovering and defining what matters most to you personally, a true, lasting type of passion and clarity is released.

26

Over the years, in numerous seminar environments, I have asked the question, "How many feel they are in a season of transition in life?" Amazingly, 75 percent respond in agreement. However, when I ask for clarity as to what the next season holds or what the plan looks like to get there, inexplicably almost none of them can describe what this transition looks like.

If you will use the following questions in a deeper, more thoughtful way, I assure you profound clarity will follow. You may find the answers are far more challenging than they may appear on the surface. Pursuing honest answers will help you envision what your life will look like in your idyllic future. As you seek the answers, you will be able to refine your understanding of what changes must occur in order to get from where you are now to where you want to go. I assure you that your core passion will build.

3C EXERCISE

At the end of each section, I have included 3C Exercises. With these, you will take the material and inspiration from the section and make it practical and actionable. Even from a casual consideration of the questions ahead, most people realize their magnitude and significance; sadly, many never take conscientious time to reflect on and answer them. The 3C Strategy for a fulfilling life will give you a framework to answer and act upon these and other of life's most important questions, using the 3C Exercises at the end of each chapter in conjunction with the free *3C Companion Guide*. The *3C Companion Guide* (available for free at www.DaveYarnes.com) has expanded material and corresponding chapter exercise questions. It is designed to give you space to reflect and comment, with exercises for further thought and application. It has a printable format designed to carry alongside this book. Consider using a notebook or journal you can keep with you as you read through the text and address the material in the 3C Exercises and *3C Companion Guide*.

The material and questions ahead make the process of actionable steps simple and rewarding. Following this plan will support you as you chart your course and own your life. You may find that having a trusted peer or life coach ask you these questions will bring out your best and truest answers for each of the 3C Exercises.

Use the *3C Companion Guide* to record your responses to these and other 3C Exercises and to journal and track your development.

- Am I in a *Clarion* or *Voyager* season?

- What really *is* most important to me? This is one of life's most profound questions. Take time to deeply reflect and describe in writing. (There is more about this in the *3C Companion Guide*.)

- What kind of person am I called to become?

- Who are the individuals I want to share my life with? What relationships are important to me? And how does this affect my time and values?

- What aspects of life are the most important to focus on in this season?

- Which area of my life is most drastically in need of improvement?

- What specific changes would I like to see?

- Can I picture myself after these changes—living in a satisfying lifestyle of fulfilment and prosperity? Write down a few statements about your future life.

Now you have some of your first and most important foundations of your individual 3C Plan. As you progress further, you can watch the plan take shape and grow into a meaningful, personalized document.

NOTE

1. Bruce Wilkinson with David and Heather Kopp, *The Dream Giver: Following Your God-Given Destiny* (Multnomah Books © 2003 Ovation Foundation).

CHAPTER 3

THE 3C STRATEGY

During my undergraduate studies, I focused on studying the inner working of the human mind in order to try to find some answers to life. I read scores of psychological resources, many of which provided some insight into this vast and amazing topic, but often they just highlighted problems and abnormalities without providing much in the way of solution. My turning point in understanding came when I started to discover principles of fulfilment. That's when I broke through to reality. In one moment, I went from passively studying information to a keen realization of how theoretical principles could be given practical application in my life in order to bring significant change.

As I mentioned earlier, I used this education to start teaching a seminar series, which became the source for much of the research and material for this book. What I learned has been invaluable in refining the core message of the Three Circle Strategy which contains the three overarching master topics. After years of research and reflection, I have found that categorizing life development within these three master topics produces sustainable progress. This view helps provide enough separation of master topics to have individual goals and strategies for each. Having three master topics keeps your strategy from being too spread out and complicated. I have received feedback from individuals who have put the 3C Strategy into practice, and some have created a category of "health and well-being" under their Self-Mastery Circle strategies and others have made a subcategory of "personal ministry" under their Spirit Circle development. The key to sustainable progress is individualizing the goals that best fit you specifically and creating measurable benchmarks to success that you can achieve with effort. As we begin to explore the 3C Strategy in depth, it's helpful to pause a moment and see the distinctions of these three circles and how they can represent your entire plan for a fulfilling life.

It has taken considerable time and effort to keep the core message simple, easy to understand, and easy to apply. In the chapters ahead, I share scenes from my personal journey. I hope these stories provide insight into my life's development and application of the 3C Strategy.

Over the past 20 years of my life, this simple but profound theme has come more and more into focus. I emphatically believe the difference between fulfilment, prosperity, and effectiveness as opposed to disappointment and scarcity is not a matter of chance but of change. My experience has led me to believe many have failed to apprehend the fulfilment and prosperity they were destined for because they lack a simple strategy.

Over many years and considerable thought, research, and refinement, the three circles, which represent the three core areas of life, emerged as the key components of making a strategy. In every individual, the areas of Spirit, Skill, and Self-Mastery embody the essential elements that need to be perfected in the journey of sustained fulfilment and prosperity. Each of these areas create overlapping circles, and, as you can see in the 3C Map, it is clear each circle is interconnected. Each area interacts and interconnects in a rewarding and fulfilling life.

INTRODUCING THE 3C MAP

Overlapping circle illustrations are often referred to as Venn Diagrams. The basic concept of the Venn diagram is to clearly convey where concepts overlap and how they interconnect. In the 3C Map, the three circles of Spirit, Skill, and Self-Mastery have overlapping areas with one another, and they represent the interconnected and interdependent relationship of these three areas. At the center, they converge like a bulls-eye on a target.

While each sphere of Spirit, Skill, and Self-Mastery has their own unique developmental designs and characteristics, which you'll read about ahead, they remain interdependent and connected to each other. How many times have you seen high-potential people have great skill, but lack the self-mastery necessary to advance their career? Or consider a highly spiritual person that has incredible character, but seems ethereal and lacks the needed skillset for useful expertise.

It's been my observation that many resources have been developed concerning the individual spheres of Spirit, Skill, and Self-Mastery, but there is little talked about or written about the holistic, harmonious nature of fulfilment and accomplishment that arises when these three circles are developed in concert with each other. In the following pages, each circle is defined in its own section, along with practical steps for growth, but for now, let's briefly discuss them on a comprehensive level.

This threefold area of life development helps in many ways. It allows you to have a specific track of development for each circle. It helps you not to neglect one or more of the circles in the long term. And it can provide encouragement, perspective, and support when you're gaining ground in one or more of the circles but perhaps having difficulty in another.

THE CIRCLE OF SPIRIT

The supremacy of the Spirit Circle places it at the top within the 3 Circle icon. I have positioned this circle at the highest point and used the image of the eternal flame to underscore the truth that you and I are more than flesh and blood. We are spiritual beings, infused in a mortal body. The goal is to grow and develop our personal spiritual life and adeptness through awareness of spiritual principles, honest personal spiritual evaluation, and meaningful implementation. This is the embodiment of the Spirit Circle.

This circle contains the seedbed of truth, hope, compassion, peace, joy, and inspiration. This circle can only be developed as you connect with the divine qualities of God.

I challenge you not to be apprehensive when we discus an ongoing spiritual relationship with God. I trust you'll find universal, transcendent truths that deeply resonate within your core being naturally. It's as though they had been there all along, waiting to be awoken. Growth in the Spirit Circle is foundational to your development within the Circles of Skill and Self-Mastery. Without this key component, even some of life's biggest accomplishments can seem hollow, unfulfilling, and unsustainable.

THE CIRCLE OF SKILLS

Learning and breathing should end at the same time. The life-long pursuit of ever-deepening skill is something that requires identification, focus, training, and experience. These abilities come from application, education and from repetition and practice. Someone once said "an expert knows more and more about less and less." Determining which skills need to be developed and how to apply them is a focus of the Skill Circle section. When you ignite your passion and chart your course, the unique, indispensable skills needed come into focus.

When you are young, you learn skills because you are under the authority of a parent or teacher at school. As you grow and mature, you need to initiate your own self-study and self-management to learn skills. The purposeful identification and development of key skills is at the core of the skill circle.

THE CIRCLE OF SELF-MASTERY

Self-Mastery is the discipline of understanding and managing your personal actions, impulses, and emotions consistently in all you do. It allows you to "feel comfortable in your own skin." It requires increasing self-awareness and self-management. In order to effectively impact and influence others as well as our environment, we must first have self-mastery.

Personal Self-Mastery is expressed in the areas of personality, inward character, and interactions with others. It includes the set of qualities that make a person distinctive, especially concerning the qualities of mind, feeling, and persona. As we grow in personal self-mastery, we can navigate interpersonal relationships with growing ease. Our ability to evaluate, influence, and persuade individuals and groups takes on new dimensions.

Due to the nature of self-awareness and self-management, the important and practical skills found in the Circle of Self-Mastery section are foundational to leadership and interaction with others.

WHY ARE THE CIRCLES INTERDEPENDENT?

This is a core concept of this book. Life is not one-dimensional. You may have already experienced a high degree of fulfilment and effectiveness in your life. There is great potential for more. You may find you have disproportionality developed a single circle. What new heights could await you? Have you ever wondered how much additional fulfilment, effectiveness, and capacity is available for you personally? There is an exponential effect when you develop all three circles of the 3C Strategy. When individuals focus mostly on the Spirit Circle, they see life as mainly mystical or ethereal. They often lack tangible personal prosperity, focused solely on spirituality without developing vital Skills and Self-Mastery.

> There is an exponential effect when you develop all three circles of the 3C Strategy.

Mastery in the development of important skills can open the door for rewarding and fulfilling accomplishments. Whether the skills are self-taught, acquired through academic pursuits, apprenticeships, or concentration and repeated application, they create a platform for some of life's most enriching accomplishments.

What about overdevelopment or disproportional development? Skills development is an important accomplishment and often the time and commitment toward mastery can be consuming. We have all learned to beware of the skilled person who is self-absorbed or arrogant in his or her own development and performance. They are blind to other areas of self-awareness and spirituality while over-focused on developing skills. This can lead to self-aggrandizement, self-promotion, and the inability to recognize that skills are a gift to benefit society. Ultimately, disproportional development minimizes comprehensive actualization.

Meaningful personal interaction and sustained ability to overcome obstacles are enabled through the Circle of Self-Mastery. Without this Circle, individuals remain at a low level of Self-Awareness and can fail to actualize. However, as important and essential as self-mastery can be, we cannot live in a state of perpetual introspection without outward action.

As you begin to learn, understand, and apply the principles in this book, it is vital to honestly evaluate what your Three Circles look like right now, and which areas in each Circle are most drastically in need of improvement. You will be able to make substantial changes immediately just by learning and applying the material. However, I have found, like many aspects of life, there are improvements in progressive layers—you add new thought processes and remove harmful ones in stages. This careful progression allows each individual to not only incorporate new skills long term, but also to "heal" from the surgical removal of harmful thought processes that were uncovered in the process of discovery and change.

The principles ahead must be coupled with your passionate and resounding determination to find new levels of personal awareness and change.

DECIDE TO START RIGHT WHERE YOU ARE

There is something about the illusion of life that the right starting point for a journey of change is somewhere ahead but not in the present hour. The right projected starting point will be "When the kids are out of school" or "After I land this new position" or "When I retire I'll have more time" or "After I finish college." The list goes on. However, the discovery of a lifetime is not somewhere far away in some vague place. Opportunities you have overlooked for years could be hidden right in front of you, waiting to be discovered. The allure of a better starting point in the future is an illusion. You only have today.

Most of the time, what you need is right in front of you, waiting to be discovered. Time and time again, men and women feel they must leave everything and seek fulfilling relationships, increased self-satisfaction, and happiness somewhere other than where they live, work, and worship. They think it is impossible that their success could be close and obtainable.

Are you like others, so convinced that satisfaction and fulfillment lies elsewhere that you may fail to see that the very thing you have been longing to uncover is within reach? I challenge you to reexamine your life and see the potential resources right at hand. Planning your passion necessitates a starting point that is always right where you're standing today.

Unimaginable discoveries are waiting for you, right under your feet. Your life, your character, your personality, your passion, and your skills are unique and fit perfectly, like a key in a lock. The experiences, richness, and quality of life that you have been seeking can all start to unfold right from where you are now.

"EUREKA MOMENTS"

The material in the following pages has been selected based on its repeated ability to produce instantaneous moments of personal revelation, which produce lasting fulfilling change. Many other aspects may need continuous course adjustment and depth of understanding that comes from consistent application of steps ahead.

I have chosen material that, in my experience, has historically produced more "Eureka Moments" than any others I have come across. A Eureka Moment is the moment when a specific topic, thought, or chapter will cause an instantaneous revelation and change. The Eureka Moment changes you positively for life. It can't be unlearned. It is the catalyst that brings you to a moment of understanding that releases true revelation. In turn, it creates a much-needed paradigm shift that alters the way you will view the world for the remainder of your years. I encourage you to enter into the next section with that expectation.

 **3C EXERCISE**

- Consider the 3C Strategy in your life. Is there one circle that is underdeveloped? Is there one that needs immediate attention?

- Which Circle (Spirit, Skill or Self-Mastery) do you feel the most reluctant to examine in your life?

- What can you do right now without procrastination to develop this area? Is there an activity you can embark on that will provide consistent growth—that class you've always wanted to take, that hobby you've wanted to learn, that spiritual journey or conference you know will be life changing?

- Is there one circle that you have over-prioritized?

- What could your life become if you had mastery in all three circles?

Reflect on and answer these and other life-changing questions in the *3C Companion Guide*. Remember that these times of reflection and the corresponding action create a practical framework to chart your course. Strive to produce actionable steps for each of the 3C Exercise sections.

CHAPTER 4

THE NEED FOR FUEL: EMOTIONAL ALIGNMENT

"I don't want to be at the mercy of my emotions. I want to use them, to enjoy them, and to dominate them."

—OSCAR WILDE

E motions fuel our movement and help create change. Positive emotions can give you clarity, drive you to persevere, and inspire others around you. Unfortunately, negative emotions are also a type of fuel. They can paralyze us from movement, cloud our judgement, and hurt us and others when they are not bridled. Before we look at the 3C Strategy and each Circle in depth, I want to discuss the key component of emotions as part of your drive and motivation, so that you are working toward your own fulfilment, prosperity, and success with sustainability.

My view on the topic of emotions and their place in our lives has changed profoundly over the years. I have come to recognize the dynamic role of emotions in fueling our efforts to find fulfilment, wealth, joy, and the things that matter most in our lives.

It takes emotion to sustain the passion to meet life's challenges. The key is *mastering* your emotions and making them work for you.

EMOTIONS ARE FUEL FOR YOUR UNIQUE 3C STRATEGY

In my early years, my examination of emotions, their roots, and their interaction in everyday life led me to a strong case for stoicism— an emotionless life. I saw emotions as something that negated logic and caused irrational behavior. I saw the presence of emotions as the absence of calculated thought and clarity. To me, emotions hindered the thinking process. From a spiritual perspective, I was concerned about some of the displays of emotion I saw in many Christian groups. I didn't feel like it was fake or inappropriate, but I questioned whether I could or should have the same type of experiences. I held this belief system and attitude until two things happened that helped radically shape my view of emotion. First, while fulfilling a requirement for my first pastorate, I was studying the New Testament when a particular verse seemed to hold my attention. Speaking of Jesus Christ, the verse stated, *"Who, in the days of His flesh, when He had offered up prayers and supplications, with vehement cries and tears to Him who was able to save Him from death, and was heard because of His godly fear"* (Hebrews 5:7).

I had always mentally pictured this scene of Christ praying as a composed, stoic prayer. But this verse shows vehement, loud cries and tears and godly fear. My mental image changed significantly after this verse stood out to me.

Also during my undergraduate years, my strongest concentration was in the field of workplace psychology—discovering what motivated people and how to acquire higher productivity out of an organization. In fulfilling this concentration, I had to spend a lot of time studying and researching abnormal psychology. I dreaded it. I would have to prepare myself mentally before I could read abnormal psychological studies. Reading the stories of broken personal lives, the overwhelming feelings I had of sympathy and compassion were hard to manage. Often, my sense of empathy for the subjects of the study was on such a personalized level, I felt as if I had some obligation toward them—I wanted to find them and help them.

I was convinced that somehow an emotional imbalance was at the core of their problems, and I thought if we could just eradicate the power of emotion in their lives, how much better off they would be. I viewed emotions as a detriment to a logic-filled life. My, how I was wrong!

I could go on for chapters about why my view of emotions has changed so drastically. However, for the purposes of our journey, I am going to cut to the chase. Emotions are fuel that allow you to take action as you ignite your passion, chart your course, and own your life. When clarity for your path is met with enthusiastic passion, and you can harness emotion, explosive change takes place.

Emotions are fuel that allow you to take action as you ignite your passion, chart your course, and own your life.

EMOTION IN SOCIETY

I am aware that many would negate the vital role of emotion because of societal misconception of the appropriateness of emotion in different social, spiritual, or professional settings.

When an individual is spiritually inspired, there can be criticism like "they're just being overly emotional." Many can be emotionally moved by a true spiritual experience, attending a performance or a religious service, or even watching a movie that inspires them to spiritual thought. It is a natural expression to be moved to tears or overwhelming joy when you are impacted by a spiritual experience or thought.

A CEO giving an impassioned presentation of a new product launch can be labeled as inappropriate, using emotion as a means to boost sales. Some would not rightly understand the emotion is linked to the years of product development and the euphoria of the final release.

Emotions are a natural, God-given, beautiful part of uncovering the treasures of personality and spiritual development within each of us. Examining moments in our lives of heightened emotion often provide clarity concerning what areas of life are uniquely important to us as individuals and in turn which areas to pursue.

EMOTIONAL INTELLIGENCE

Emotional Intelligence (EQ) is a term used to describe a mature level of emotional balance. EQ is the measure of how much you understand and master your emotions and identify and adjust to the emotions of others. EQ is often a greater indicator for predicting who will be a high performer, more so even than IQ or technical skills. It's amazing how the study of emotional intelligence has risen from a few articles beginning around 1990 to a significant field of study complete with a wealth of books, articles, and university courses today.

Increasing levels of maturity in emotional intelligence are similar to increasing levels of Self-Mastery. The first step begins with Emotional Self-Awareness. The degree to which you become aware of how your emotions look to others is a step toward increasing your emotional intelligence. Think of the last time you witnessed someone behaving in an emotionally unacceptable manner. In most instances, the individual displaying the behavior is unaware of their emotional state and how they are being perceived by others. How about a boss, leader, or statesman who delivers directives with a passionless, disengaged emotional quality, do we follow them?

NONVERBAL EMOTIONAL EXPRESSIONS

When two people have a face-to-face conversation, they exchange not only words, but also voice inflections and nonverbal cues. They communicate with tone of voice, posture, facial expression, and eye contact.

Research validates that there is far more information being exchanged on a nonverbal level during the average conversation than the verbal level—more than we have ever imagined. The amount of nonverbal information exchanged in a face-to-face conversation far outshadows the literal spoken conversation.

As human beings, we are able to interoperate with nonverbal cues. The significance of nonverbal cues, as it has been studied over the years, has a greater influence on our interactions than was initially believed. In conversation, we are very adept at ascribing meaning to cues in others. We give off what I call "white noise" during our interactions—a simple hand gesture, shift in posture, brief facial expression, or even the way we change our breathing is picked up by others as we communicate. Our nonverbal emotional cues often betray what we are truly feeling about what we are communicating. The "feeling" the speaker radiates is often more important than the content of the conversation. Becoming increasingly aware of this nonverbal communication and endeavoring to use it to our benefit has significant impact on our effectiveness.

To increase effectiveness with nonverbal communication, your internal views have to passionately align with your subject matter. This is exemplified in the phase "more is caught than taught." The next time you're communicating in person, check to make sure you are internally aligned with the content. Take time to adjust either your content or attitude as needed. Then you'll be in a far greater persuasive position.

EMOTIONAL FEAR CAN KILL ADVANCEMENT

If you were to keep a detailed record of the various thoughts and emotions that go through your mind in a week's time and arrange them categorically, you may be astounded to see how many of your thoughts are wrapped around fears, especially fear of things that never come to pass! Certainly, there are instances where fear is a heathy appropriate response. To actualize, we need to distinguish between legitimate fear and fear that causes dysfunction.

MASTERING THE EMOTION OF FEAR

In order for an object to be legitimately fearful, it has to possess two distinct characteristics. *It has to be present, and it has to be potent.*

If a woman, sitting in an office, is suddenly afraid of a spider, her fear may or may not be legitimate.

If her fear is based on the thought of a spider that is not present, then we could say she has a phobia or paranoia, and her fear is not legitimate.

If there is a spider present, but it is a toy spider that has surprised her, that fear is based on an object that is *present*, but because the spider is fake, it lacks *potency*. The fear is still not legitimate.

However, if the spider she encountered was both real and poisonous, having both *presence* and *potency*, then her fear would be legitimate.

Many people spend vast amounts of time in worry and anxiety over fears that are neither present nor potent. For them, fear is emotional fuel driving them in the wrong direction.

- Fears can cause people to avoid social situations that could advance their career.

- Fears may prevent entrepreneurs or investors from taking risks that could lead to enormous achievement.

- Fears can keep us from healthy change.

- Fear is the enemy of creativity.

- Fearful emotions can be transmitted to others, causing them to react to us in undesired ways.

Your fears can become ties that bind you and keep you doing things that are safe and familiar. They can hinder you from exploration and change. Fear will keep you from stepping out and taking risks that produce change and unleash the potential for fulfilment and prosperity in your life. Fears and anxieties can be so deeply rooted that even when you are enjoying great success, your state of mind doesn't allow you to take the needed time to recognize and celebrate the accomplishment. Decide now to reject illegitimate fear as you change to: ignite your passion, chart your course, and own your fulfilling and prosperous life.

FEAR AND ROOT NEGATIVE EMOTIONS

Think of a young person who overheard their parents continually arguing about money throughout their childhood. Over time, that person could develop deep-rooted negative emotions associated with the topic of money. Their painful emotional links could cause them to avoid legitimate conversations about finances and keep them from being as successful as they could be. If left unchecked, these negative emotions can produce what some call self-sabotage. Behavior is deemed self-sabotaging when it thwarts us from a path of success, creates problems, or diverts us from our desired goals.

If we connect positive emotions to negative habits, they can also be used to reinforce unproductive habits. When I was young, my mother would often answer all of my life's disappointments by cooking or baking something for me. Over the years, eating when I was emotionally down became a habit loop. My emotional mind associated the comfort of food with the love, nurturing, and affirmation of my mother. It's easy to see the importance of recognizing and changing these emotional connections. Learn to recognize and reject illegitimate fear, and self-sabotaging emotion.

 **3C EXERCISE**

- Can you identify times when your "nonverbal alignment" has been recognized by others?

- What has been your view of emotions and their role in your life? Does your view need adjustment?

- In the past, have your emotions helped or hindered your progress in obtaining life's most important goals?

- What are some of the lingering fears in your life? Are they legitimate? What personal measures can you take to overcome them?

- How can you begin to use your emotions as fuel for your dreams?

- What thoughts keep you from healthy displays of emotion?

By now, your *3C Companion Guide* is starting to become an important resource for review of the answers to these and other important questions. If you haven't started using the *3C Companion Guide,* please consider it. It is available to download for free at www.DaveYarnes.com.

CHAPTER 5

CIRCLE OF THE SPIRIT

"We don't have a soul. We are
a soul. We have a body."
C.S. LEWIS

As I was working at my first significant job after college, something happened that changed the course of my life and my understanding about personal and spiritual development. I was working under a contract for the New York State Department of Economic Development, analyzing New York's export strategy and assisting the business headquartered in the state. This was during the late 80s and early 90s, and New York State had some of the largest export traffic in the world through companies like IBM, Kodak, Xerox, and others. New York's proximity to Canada and large port system made the state one of the busiest in worldwide export traffic. Our central office was in Manhattan, and I would make trips there from my home near Buffalo. I learned so much during these years; I was analyzing around 100 businesses a year, many by traveling to each site to perform the analysis. The training and experience I received has become the foundation for my entrepreneurial career. The more I met with and analyzed successful companies, the more I was eager to develop my own.

During those years, I became acquainted with a ministry that had a homeless outreach in Times Square, Manhattan. In the late 80s and early 90s, Times Square was a sordid place. It was before the big cleanup that Mayor Giuliani initiated, and Times Square had a great deal of drug trafficking, homeless population, prostitution, and crime. A group of friends introduced me to the ministry and its goal of helping some of the most desperate and marginalized people in the area to find sobriety, hope, and a path to a healthy lifestyle.

The ministry organization leased an upper floor of a series of buildings directly across from the Port Authority bus station in Mid-town, Manhattan, placing them near the heart of Times Square in an area known as Hell's Kitchen. After my 9-to-5 work was done in the city, I would volunteer. Assisting mostly in the evenings and on the weekend, I always felt a very rewarding and enriched sense of purpose. My volunteer assignment was to walk through the area and personally invite homeless people, drug addicts, and the like to come to an evening meeting where there would be coffee, a hot meal, and some straight talk about getting out of addiction, prostitution, and drug abuse. My assignment was an important part of the process, because the community we were trying to affect would only learn about meetings and social programs through word of mouth. Each night at these meetings, we had speakers who were once prostitutes or drug addicts come and give their powerful testimonials—they spoke about how they were ordinary people who had tried everything to live a purposeful life but could not break their addictive and destruc-tive lifestyles before they had an encounter with God. This was the most important and effective strategy in reaching this group. These desperate, marginalized people would hear the firsthand stories of overcoming addiction and breaking through enormous obstacles, and it gave hope and direction like nothing else. After they shared, there would often be numerous people emotionally impacted who wanted to know how to make the steps necessary for change.

As I look back at these meetings, they were probably best described as a hybrid of a soup kitchen, an AA meeting, and a church service. Their effectiveness was tremendous. They consistently had testimonies of sustained recovery and long-lasting impact that reached numbers many times that of government-run facilities.

One hot July summer night, I was combing through a community of homeless people who had taken refuge under one of the large overpasses that made up the bus terminal. There were cardboard boxes made into little shelters, bags of garbage and piles of clothes that obviously belonged to the inhabitants of the shelters, and scattered throughout this landscape were hundreds of homeless men and women. I remember clearly to this day striking up a conversation with a homeless man whose name was Richard; he was about ten years older than me, in his late 30s or early 40s, and had been homeless on the streets of Midtown for many years. I had spoken with dozens of individuals that night already, but there was something about our conversation that seemed to connect more than the others. From where we stood, I could point to the building where our meetings and the food distribution would soon start. I asked him, to come and check it out. I told him that I would wait and take a seat by the door so I could help him find his way inside. After a bit of reluctance, he told me that he would be there.

That night, as I waited by the door, a stream of some of the most broken, sick, and addicted people I'd ever seen in my life brushed past me on their way in to have a hot meal, a cup of coffee, and hear that evening's speaker. The heat wave that had been going through New York made the stench from the city streets, and many of the people coming in, almost unbearable. The mass of desperate people coming in were from all ages and walks of life. I saw young prostitutes that were jaundiced and yellow with hepatitis and elderly homeless people that were destitute. As I watched the people coming through the door, I wondered how long they could live in their present condition.

I half expected that Richard wouldn't make it. But you can imagine how delighted I was when I saw him coming up the stairs. The thing that struck me first was the size and thickness of the coat that he was wearing. It reminded me of something you would wear in a winter blizzard, not a sweltering summer night. He also clutched a clear plastic bag under his coat that seem to be about the size of a large bed pillow.

I greeted Richard, and he seemed genuinely happy to see me. We came inside, and I helped him find a seat. I took the seat next to him and talked to him about the length of the service and how to get a meal afterwards. Once he was seated, I went to get him a cup of coffee and came back just in time to hear the evening speaker begin. It was very hot in that upper room, and I asked Richard if I could take his coat and hang it up. Immediately, I saw the fear flash in his eyes. I realized that his coat and the bag that he was carrying contained all the valuables in his life. When he had agreed to leave his cardboard box to join me, he had to take anything of perceived value with him so that it wouldn't be stolen during his absence. He took his coat off and set it on the chair between us and kept his hand tight on the plastic bag as he set that between us as well.

The man who started to speak was a former heroin addict from that part of Manhattan who had turned his life around and was telling his story and the keys to his recovery. At different points, he would make reference to a Bible passage. At one point, I noticed Richard looking around at people thumbing through Bibles with an inquisitive look. In response, I opened the Bible that I had to the scripture the speaker was referring to and began to pass it towards Richard. As I did, my hands brushed over the top of his plastic bag that he held tightly between us. When he noticed me reaching toward him, he wrenched back and pulled the bag toward him tightly. I was shocked. At first I didn't understand, but then it became clear he saw my movement as a potential threat of theft of his bag. I tried to assure him that wasn't the case and made another attempt at passing him my Bible. This was too much. He wrenched back again, pulled his possessions to the other side of his body so it was no longer next to me, and he completely shut down any further communication with me. I was stunned. I could see the entire contents through the clear grimy bag. It contained a few empty cans he was going to turn in for deposit money, some very dirty clothes, and what looked like less than a dollar in change.

This situation was so disconcerting for me. I thought to myself, "God, this man is missing an opportunity to radically transform his life. He's missing the ability for the first time to see a Bible and its contents. He is so distracted that he is also missing any instructions on how to get further help from this organization." Richard's eyes were wild and frantic. When there was a break in the meeting, he snatched up his bag and coat and headed for the door.

I was heartbroken. It felt to me that this may be one of his last chances for change and a better life. He was so close to help, but the contents of his bag, which contained nothing of value that you and I would ever want, was the sole obstacle keeping him from a life of sanity, sobriety, and fulfillment.

I pondered this deeply and emotionally. In the next moment, something happened that is still, to this day, very emotional and difficult to explain. In a word, I felt an overwhelming sense of the *presence* of God. It was surprising and unexpected. The words that I heard were not audible, but profoundly clear.

"Son, in your life you will also have possessions—houses, cars, bank accounts, and many things that will be precious from your perspective. But never think that they are any different or more valuable than those rags in Richard's bag. If they keep you from hearing and fulfilling My direction for your life, they are worthless."

From that moment on, my view of living a fulfilling life was transformed. I understood with clarity these words of Jesus Christ, *"For what profit is it to a man if he gains the whole world, and loses his own soul? Or what will a man give in exchange for his soul"* (Matthew 16:26)

I was conscious that my possessions, and the self-focus they could bring, could hold me back from a truly fulfilling life. Small-minded,

> Small-minded, temporal values can distract us from grasping meaningful and fulfilling insights and direction.

temporal values can distract us from grasping meaningful and fulfilling insights and direction. I have never forgotten that look on Richard's face when he clutched his bag of belongings and could not leave it behind to find a better life. If I find myself holding my own businesses or profits a little too close, I think back to that moment and I remind myself that my possessions will never hold me back from living a God-directed fulfilling life.

PREEMINENCE OF THE SPIRIT CIRCLE

The preeminence of the Spirit Circle can't be overstated. Within the 3 Circle icon, we have positioned this circle on top and have used the image of the eternal flame as its symbol. At the center of the Spirit Circle is a foundational truth that you and I are more than flesh and blood. We are spiritual beings infused in a mortal body. For now, this infusion makes it impossible to fully dissect the natural from the spiritual until death, when the two will finally become distinct. This is not a call to religion as most would define it. For our purposes, this is much more personal and individualized.

Very few things are common across all audiences and all cultures. I believe there are three desires that are shared by everyone. We all have a need to be loved. We all want our lives to matter and count for something. We all possess an eternal component that longs to connect with God. Without this last spiritual connection, other pursuits become hollow and lack meaning.

Every person I have ever met wants their life to be significant and impactful. I have also observed, no matter how successful that person's life is or how vast their accomplishments are, without a meaningful spiritual connection, their life is somehow empty.

KNOWLEDGE, WISDOM, AND UNDERSTANDING

You did not evolve from meaningless, base elements of this earth—you were created. Your connection with your creator is foundational for a life of impact and meaning, a life of fulfilment and significance. The apostle Paul, a central character of the Bible's New Testament, prayed for a group of friends, and his prayer is forever recorded in cannon scripture. His prayer from that ancient time still, to this day, concisely captures the preeminence of knowing and aligning our lives with the will of God. His prayer is found in Colossians 1:9-10: *"For this reason we also, since the day we heard it, do not cease to pray for you, and to ask that you may be filled with the knowledge of His will in all wisdom and spiritual understanding; that you may walk worthy of the Lord, fully pleasing Him, being fruitful in every good work and increasing in the knowledge of God."*

There are several aspects in this short passage that are important and worth taking a moment to analyze. First, the Apostle Paul asks that his friends be "filled" with the knowledge of God's will for their lives. This assumes that this knowledge is not automatic. Paul's heartfelt desire is that they become "filled," suggesting that large degrees of knowledge and clarity are obtainable. He also continues to ask that this filling would come with knowledge, wisdom, and understanding. He closes this section by saying that once they have and apply this understanding of God's will, they will live life in a "worthy manner," be pleasing to God, and be fruitful for every good work.

Intuitively, each of us senses that we possess eternal attributes. Whether this is defined as a soul or a spirit, universally there is a sense of an eternal component that connects us to God. I find it remarkable how few resources allow for spiritual alignment as a core part of life planning.

> Intuitively, each of us senses that we possess eternal attributes

My doctoral work is concentrated around biblical studies. Although I don't presume to be an expert, much of my life has been devoted to biblical reading, research, and presentation. One simple concept I believe fits the entirety of my research more than any other—the grace of God. From the beginning of the Bible to the end, I believe that "grace" is the overarching theme. Jesus Christ Himself, as He walked this earth, not only taught about the subject but modeled it in the flesh.

So what is this grace of God? Why is it important in developing a fulfilling life? It's more than just forgiveness; God gives His best without regard to our performance. Grace is the most important central idea in the Bible, Christianity, and all of God's world. Grace is the love of God shown to the undeserving and ungrateful. Grace is His peace, blessing, and unmerited favor given freely to all who seek it. In grace, God gives nothing less than the entirety of Himself. The man Christ Jesus is the embodiment of grace. (Please download my free *Spiritual Life Application Guide* from www.DaveYarnes.com for more detail on the subject.)

Throughout the ages, God's true nature was shrouded until He came, Himself, in the form of Jesus Christ to tell us the nature of our Father God. In the remarkable depiction of the prodigal son, Jesus Christ tells the story of a man who had two sons. One took his inheritance and consumed it on a debaucherous lifestyle. Once it was all spent he came back home to his father. Expecting to be chastised, ridiculed, and demoted to the point of a slave. Christ Jesus gives us an intimate depiction of the grace of God through the father's response to this wayward son. Consider this scene from the book of Luke, which I feel is one of the most remarkable depictions of God's grace:

> And he arose and came to his father. But when he was still a great way off, his father saw him and had compassion, and ran and fell on his neck and kissed him. And the son said to him, "Father, I have sinned against heaven and in your sight, and am no longer worthy to be called your son."

> But the father said to his servants, "Bring out the best robe and put it on him, and put a ring on his hand and sandals on his feet. And bring the fatted calf here and kill it, and let us eat and be merry; for this my son was dead and is alive again; he was lost and is found." And they began to be merry (Luke 15:20-24).

While he was a long way off, the father went to him, lavished the best of his household on him, forgave him, and welcomed him back as a son and appointed him to the highest honor he could. This is a picture for all of us of the grace of God. None are beyond His reach.

This is also a profound understanding of God giving us His best when we have no ability to deserve it. The grace of God is neither earned nor deserved; it comes through the realization and personal application of the life, death, burial, and resurrection of Christ Jesus. Simply believing in Christ, His sacrifice, and inviting Him to be master of my life atones for my sin. There's no catechism to follow, no rituals that I can perform, and no act of service that merits this. It is solely based on the grace of God. This grace further launches me into a life of meaning and purpose where I am connected with God in a way that is intimately beyond the realm of this physical world. His love and compassion, and the desire for my betterment, is beyond human compare.

As we talk about the Spirit Circle, keep this as the foremost thought: the loving, forgiving, restoring grace of God is available to each one of us through the sacrifice, death, and resurrection of His Son, Jesus Christ. There is no other topic in psychology, human history, or personal development that remotely compares.

MOST HIGH AND MOST NIGH GOD

As a child, I remember in grade school being introduced to the reality that the universe is infinite. This was a big thought and a little overwhelming. Simultaneously, there was a deep internal realization that somehow I was connected to this infinite universe. I knew this intuitively. As one person put it, "there was eternity in my heart."

Since that time as a small child, when I developed an understanding of God, I have learned the God of the universe is powerful, infinite, and vast beyond human comprehension. His nature is that of purity and holiness, yet somehow, further, God has great love. He exudes intimate knowledge and care for His creation. Even though God has incomprehensible authority, God is deeply interested in the smallest affairs of my life. So how does spiritual life develop? Like all aspects of our life, we grow into it.

You don't have to be a devout religious person to grow and flourish spiritually. As I understand it, religion focuses on our outward response to God. This can take the form of regular attendance to a church service or a Mass or one of many great spiritual expressions of our personal worship and faith. These have an important place in our lives and our culture, but there is something much deeper than our outward expression. Beyond the "corporate" relationship with God, there is the more intimate and personal understanding of God's principles and direction for life, along with my acknowledgement, alignment, and response to God. You don't have to be overly educated in spiritual matters to have this personal connection to God. It begins by understanding universal spiritual truths that influence and shape ourselves and our world. Faith, gratitude, and reciprocity are just a few. Prayer, meditation, and contemplation are often our response to these spiritual truths.

Where is the starting point to this deeper spiritual alignment? It begins at the point of conversion. This is perhaps the most profound concept in all of human history. Spiritual scholars, priests, poets, and writers have devoted centuries to this understanding. The materials written concerning personal conversion fill libraries and universities around the world.

Conversion happens at a singular point in time. Many cannot recall the exact date or time, but there in fact was one. We are born with a spiritual nature. Our spiritual nature from the time we are young, however, lacks one important event to allow spiritual transformation—an act of our will, the sovereign use of our volition to choose.

The point of spiritual conversion has different terminology in different cultures and varying expressions of faith and religion. Some may call this "finding God," "conversion," "spiritually awakened," "rebirth," or "being born again." I believe the reason there is varying terminology is that personal conversion is so profound that we lack human ability to fully describe it. The account of Jesus Christ in the gospel of John gives simple clarity.

> There was a man of the Pharisees named Nicodemus, a ruler of the Jews. This man came to Jesus by night and said to Him, "Rabbi, we know that You are a teacher come from God; for no one can do these signs that You do unless God is with him."
>
> Jesus answered and said to him, "Most assuredly, I say to you, unless one is born again, he cannot see the kingdom of God" (John 3:1-3).

The conversation between Jesus Christ and Nicodemus the Pharisee provides a clear picture of the necessity of conversion and how it differs from religious observance. Nicodemus was a highly educated lifetime practitioner of his religion. The life of a Pharisee was one of painstaking observance to religious edicts; from clothing and diet to constant study of spiritual material, he was an extremely devout man. Yet in this conversation, he struggles to grasp the simple truth, that in order to be truly spiritual, there has to be a point of conversion. In each individual life, our God has endowed us with free will. No matter what my outward religious observance is, I have to come to a point of true spiritual conversion that enables a new spiritual life.

THE BEGINNING OF MY SPIRITUAL JOURNEY

For me, true spiritual conversion took place one night when I was about 18 years old. I had very little formative spiritual background. That one evening, almost 40 years ago, changed my life and my very existence forever. I was standing outside of a small local bar, talking with a man I had never met before. There was something so significantly different about him that I was drawn to his conversation. After getting to know each other for a minute or two, I told him that I saw something in him that I desperately wanted and needed. He said to me, "You may have tried meditation or other external observances of religion, but you're missing something and it is more important than you'll ever know—you must be born again." He went on to explain to me in very simple terms the foundation of Christian faith.

I had lived my life up until that point apart from God. My life and the mistakes and sins I committed and my very nature caused me to be self-reliant and separate from a spiritual connection with God's Spirit. Although I had never heard the words this man had spoken before, I knew them to be truth of the highest level. No one had to convince me I needed God to come in to my very being and turn on the light where there had been only darkness and emptiness. I knew that my whole life needed to be transformed. It happened that evening. With a very simple prayer, I used my own will and volition and said something like this:

"God, I want You to rule over my being and my nature. I realize that I've been living a self-reliant life and that many of the actions and sins that I've committed have been displeasing to You and have been hurtful to others. Even though I don't fully understand, I know that You provided a sacrifice and an entry point for me through the birth, death, burial, and resurrection of Jesus Christ. Forgive me. Please come and live in me now. I want to be a new creature."

There are few points in my life that I can look back to with any comparison of the significance of that night. I went from being temporal and mortal to possessing the eternal life of God. I went from darkness to light. There were many habits and mindsets that needed to be changed, corrected, and abandoned over time, but there was never another day on this earth that I was the same being. I literally, from that point on, possessed the spiritual nature of God within me. (If you have not had this experience, I urge you to download the free, *Spiritual Life Application Guide* from www.DaveYarnes.com and begin a new life.)

Your development of this area is transcendent, existing outside the material plane and so not limited by it. This part of life contains the seedbed of truth: hope, compassion, peace, joy, and inspiration. It helps us to differentiate between the temporal and things of eternal value. This area is developed as you connect with the divine qualities in yourself, God, and others.

Without the Spirit Circle, this book is just about human psychology and skill development. As important as these two components are, they cannot take us to our highest destiny on their own. We could miss the experience of true fulfilment that comes from a true spiritual connection and inspiration. Through spiritual enlightenment, we gain ultimate perspective and new awareness of the purpose for life.

HOW AA FOSTERS CHANGE

Change is hard. Change without God is often impossible. Perhaps the most noted and most influential of institutions to understand the role of the Spirit Circle and its influence in creating powerful change is Alcoholics Anonymous (AA). I don't believe there is another single institution, cathedral, or temple that can lay claim to the amount and depth of changed lives to the degree AA can.

Advanced alcoholism is a debilitating and cancerous condition that drastically affects not only the life of the individual but also all of their personal interactions. For centuries, the unbearable effects of alcoholism were thought to be incurable. However, in 1935 in Akron, Ohio, Bill W. (a New York stockbroker) and Dr. Bob S. (an Akron surgeon) achieved lasting sobriety.[1] They had both been long-time, hopeless alcoholics, but they were miraculously able to reach and maintain an alcohol-free lifestyle. Their highest goal became to help others along this path.

Change without God is often impossible.

They established the steps and concepts that would eventually be developed into AA. As part of their process, there was no church to join or catechism to follow, not even the simplest definition of religious context. Instead, they emphasized the simplistic approach to acknowledging a personal connection to a higher power. I encourage you to adopt this approach as you develop this component of life.

Millions of lives have been transformed through AA, going from failure to fulfillment through their steps. The first three steps focus on spiritual truths and connections to universal spiritual principles; they are simple, easy to apply, and profoundly transformative:

1. I admit I am powerless over alcohol—that my life has become unmanageable.

2. I believe that a power greater than myself could restore me to sanity.

3. I make the decision to turn my will and my life over to the care of God as I understand Him.[2]

THE COMMON STORY

As I interact with thousands each year who often share their story of personal transformation, I am amazed at how many state an identical narrative concerning the discovery of spiritual truths. Although the stories may have different characters and various conditions, they closely follow a similar plot line. It goes something like this "I was helpless, at the end of my rope; I felt I had reached rock bottom. At that time, I felt an irresistible force telling me there was a God. I cried out to God, even though I didn't fully understand or believe, and my life radically changed forever."

The areas of desperation change. Sometimes there is an addiction, sometimes there is a loss of family, other times it's financial collapse, but whatever drives the individual to this desperation, the heart of change becomes the deep acknowledgment of the need for God. When all human effort has failed, there is the ultimate surrender and appeal to God.

When we come to a point of deepest despair and desperation, this condition creates clarity that strips away any desire for trite or superficial answers. Maybe your life is not ravaged by alcohol, but are there other areas beyond your ability to change? Is it your marriage? Another addiction or habit to which you are powerless? For many, it might be a sense of emptiness and lack of true meaning, direction, and purpose in life. Maybe deeper fulfilment, peace, and direction, have evaded you.

Innermost fulfilment, more than you have ever imagined, starts with the three simple steps, similar to AA. One, we admit that without spiritual help, we are powerless over certain aspects of our lives. Two, we believe that a power, a divine influence that is greater than ourselves can lead us to true, lasting, fulfilling lives. Three, we make a decision to align our lives with divinely-inspired truths we discover through this humble acknowledgement. We begin to shape our lives cooperatively with a spiritual connection to God.

Let me say emphatically, you do not have to reach rock bottom before this spiritual acknowledgement and transformation takes place. You can start today. Often, our pride and self-reliance keep us from this simple conclusion: you need God's help. It just seems, unfortunately, that it takes dramatic events before this becomes our conclusion.

DEFINITION OF ACCOMPLISHMENT IN THE SPIRIT CIRCLE

The definition of success in the Spirit Circle is different from the other circles. Success here opens the opportunity for success in every other arena of life. In the Spirit Circle, God interacts. This interaction creates the supernatural environment where your spirit can develop. In this transcendent realm, free from the constraints of the material universe, you can remain unshaken by daily challenges as you build your skills and develop your character. Your prosperity and fulfilment take on new dimensions and definitions. When all around you is in turmoil and no one knows where to go, you are the one with the wisdom, peace, and stability to lead the way. This comes from your strong spiritual development.

SPIRITUAL STRENGTHS

From the time you became able to comprehend direction from others, your early years of life were centered on strengthening areas of personal weakness. You were assisted in your development from birth by caregivers who, for your own survival, begin to teach you how to grow out of your weaknesses.

> *We all have a driving need to connect with God spiritually. Without this connection, the other pursuits can become meaningless.*

As you grew, you moved from learning basic survival and locomotive skills to discovering a world of information and tasks you knew nothing about. From the encouragement to walk and develop as an infant, to lessons at grammar school, all of your early education was centered on strengthening your weaknesses.

Sometime during these years, you became aware that you no longer needed to focus on areas of weakness, but it was time to develop your strengths. The Spirit Circle is where you identify and build on your unique spiritual giftings or strengths.

Most people do not have a plan for developing their spiritual strengths. Individuals have strong spiritual capacity in a similar way that they can have strong physical or mental attributes. You may have strengths in compassion, intuition, kindness, encouragement, or strength for sharing your faith. You may have spiritual strengths that allow you to sense the needs of others around you. Discovering these strengths and engaging in activities that develop these strengths is the practical application of the Spirit Circle in the 3C Strategy.

Imagine a seven-foot high school student with a love for basketball who knows he has no skill or passion for other sports. If he neglected developing his strong basketball skills because he spent time trying to do better in other sports, like bowling or gymnastics, we would think he was wasting his potential. In most high schools, there are entire classes devoted to high-performance thinkers so they can invest more time in developing their already high-level intelligence. This is something that we should also be doing in the spiritual arena. We should discover our strengths at an early age and work on developing those strengths and finding the environment where we will thrive.

I believe a plan to find that place where your spiritual strengths flourish is vitally important. There are all kinds of plans for personal spiritual development. You need to create the one that fits best for you. I have made portions of my personal spiritual plan and the fundamental belief behind it available at, www.DaveYarnes.com in my free resource the *Spiritual Life Application Guide*. I am passionate about my beliefs, but I only share them as a source of reference. You must develop your own individualized plan.

MAKE A PLAN

Like other areas of life, I highly recommend developing a customized personal spiritual plan. Without some focus, priority, and intentionality, the 3C Spirit Circle can be the first area of life to be neglected. Life is busy and often filled with distraction. Don't get so caught up in the cares, worries, and business of life and fail to develop its most important components.

Your plan could include a daily time of quiet contemplation and reflection on God and His divine attributes, a time of truthful conversation or prayer, or a journal of your progress and understandings. Importantly, you might develop a list of activities you feel divinely inspired to participate in, like reading an uplifting spiritual book. You could set aside time for helping and showing compassion to others, such as visiting a homeless shelter or a nursing home for the sole purpose of showing compassion. A spiritual plan can help you become free from anxiety, and your life can take on a new purpose. You may have been a long-time practitioner of these or similar activities or this may be the first time you have decided to provide the needed time or attention to spiritual growth. Avoid comparison with others. You are spiritually unique and your 3C Spirit Plan is bound to be unique.

A spiritual plan can help you become free from anxiety, and your life can take on a new purpose.

Through this process, continued spiritual enlightenment takes place. There comes a response in our pursuit; we call to God and He answers. Whether through divine intervention, a peaceful inner voice, miraculous circumstance, or a small ever-increasing sense of God's presence, He responds and guides.

YOUR SPIRIT AND YOUR MIND

Your internal thought life moves at an astounding rate of 600–700 words per minute. It takes proactive steps to focus this rigorous state of mind on working to your advantage. The mind is continuously being filled, either passively or actively, by influences that surround you at any given moment. Your mind and Spirit are interconnected and both are nourished by what you focus on.

I cannot overstate the importance of recognizing that every day you are being educated and your mind is being filled with something, whether you consciously choose it or not. You are either selecting the content and actively controlling your thoughts by a process I call "Active Meditation," or you're allowing your mind to be overrun by outside influences. It is important to take the time to consider your thoughts and to learn how to manage what you allow to fill your mind and affect your spirit.

MEDITATION PRACTICES THAT STRENGTHEN OUR MIND

There are several different views when it comes to managing the mind which in turn affects your spirit. Some of these practices are detrimental. One example is mind-emptying, which is a familiar concept at the root of many occult practices. I don't believe chasing out negatives and blanking out our minds is a helpful process.

I do believe the concept of mind renewal and "Active Meditation" significantly aids fulfilment and true prosperity.

You are responsible for all actions related to the control center of your thought life. This should be guarded as it touches your Spirit Circle. You should never abdicate control of your mind, will, or emotions. If you do, it is a starting point for disorienting thoughts. An empty mind with no self-management can have negative side effects, such as confusion, burdens of fear, and disorientation.

Without strengthening the mind by actively filling it, the control and volition of the mind begins to weaken and atrophy. This can happen through neglect, or even simply indulging in too much media or entertainment. I believe there is an actual loss of natural intelligence when the mind is not actively strengthened.

God gave each person sovereignty over their minds. Spiritual betterment of your mind is a process of actively filling it more and more with right thoughts as opposed to passive entertainment or blanking it out for the sake of a mystical spiritual experience. This is a critical differentiation.

ACTIVELY FILLING THE MIND

Your mind needs to be constantly renewed and fed. This in turn nourishes your spirit. Your focus should be a lifetime journey, filled with true fulfilment and prosperity, characterized by healthy spiritual growth. You are the vigilant guard over your mind. Imagine guards at the gate of an ancient fortified city who momentarily hold captive, at the point of a spear, every traveler, tradesman, or foreigner who tries to enter the city. These guards carefully inspect all baggage and motivations before allowing entry through the gate.

If left unguarded, the mind will be filled with whatever is readily passing through your life at any given moment. Entertainment and social media can be great sources of information and inspiration, but they can also be a waste of precious time, or worse, they can give place to negative thoughts, fears, greed, and the like. Stray thoughts will, at best, just keep you from peace of mind and may even lead to losing focus on your passions for the future. The process of taking every thought captive is to actively choose what to focus on and also to actively decide what sources are not worth your time.

I have found it especially helpful not to overthink or wrongly interpret correspondence. Jack receives an email from Ray but it is short and the tone is direct. If Jack is not careful, his mind can quickly turn negative. "Ray didn't like what I had to say, and now he's angry, how can I fix this?" Nine times out of ten, you misinterpret and enable negative unproductive thought streams. Chances are Ray was just in a hurry and didn't reread his email.

ACTIVELY MANAGED MEDITATION

Your mind is a vacuum waiting to be filled with healthy thoughts. I am convinced that the way to fill a healthy mind, and in turn positively charge your spirit, is to undertake an active process of filling it with good things—satiating it purposefully and actively. This is an active mind process, not a passive one. It is a curriculum designed by you under the authority and inspiration of God. In this active process, negative aspects become diluted and you receive amazing, positive benefits.

Take active authority over the condition of your spirit

Take active authority over the condition of your spirit. Make a plan for daily Active Meditation. Active Meditation seeks to fill your mind with good, pure, and honorable things such as thinking about the loving aspects of God, imagining your future accomplishments, or believing for a life that contributes and benefits others. When we rehearse these and imprint them, positive thoughts become second nature, even when you are met by negative challenges. This, in turn, produces an abundant soul or inner spiritual connection to God.

Mind-enhancement practices that come from popular sources, fads, or quick-fix schemes often lack essential spiritual principles for sustainable fulfilment. They can be harmful and fall heavily into two ditches.

1. They pervert the search for true fulfilling prosperity by stirring up greed-based motivations (money, power, things).

2. They lean heavily on dangerous mysticism and occult practices that call you to empty your mind and relinquish personal sovereignty and proactivity.

SPIRITUAL FORCES

I'd like to share a very personal story that illustrates the transcendent, miraculous nature of our spiritual connection with God through Christ Jesus. About 20 years ago, I began working to help orphans of parents who died from AIDS in East Africa. The disease had spread to a pandemic state. We encountered whole villages where almost all the adult population had died. The need for orphan care was overwhelming.

During our travels, we happened upon a site that was one of the most dismal I had seen. There was a single adult overseer, affectionately called "Mama Grace," who was taking care of approximately 70 orphans ranging in age from 1 to 15 years old. Most of the children had come from a nearby village decimated by HIV. Some of the children were literally left as babies on the doorstep of the main building. The orphanage had received some initial funds from an American organization, but soon after the initial purchase of the land and constructing a few small primitive buildings, the funding stopped and their financial backers disappeared. I had seen this scenario before. The excitement surrounding the effort to help impoverished children wanes once the realization of continuous care until adulthood becomes apparent.

What remained on this site were four or five primitively built huts and three or four metal buildings that were largely unfinished, mostly with dirt floors. Makeshift classroom desks and dorm-style housing occupied the rooms. Their food supply on my first visit was completely depleted. We scurried to get our hands on as much food and supplies as we could to help the situation. During my first overnight stay, which was in a small mud hut on the property, I sat down and began to ask Mama Grace about how her time had been in recent months. She was unusually upbeat and joyful. She talked about the children, and she downplayed the lack of food and nutrition because of embarrassment, then she said something that I had no grid for. I had asked her how things had been in the last few weeks. Her response was remarkable.

She said, "It's been so much better since Jesus came last Tuesday at 10 PM." Although we were both speaking English, I immediately felt I had misunderstood her response, so I asked her for more detail. She repeated, "Things are so much better since Jesus came last Tuesday at 10 PM." I circled back and asked her what that experience was like; her response was unbelievable. She said at 10 PM, the children were in bed in one of three corresponding buildings (the older boys had one small building, as did the older girls; the younger children were helped by some of the older girls and Mama Grace). I had toured these buildings earlier. They were overcrowded with three-level bunkbeds stacked high, taking up almost all of the floor space. Sometimes children were packed into two children per bunk. She said at exactly 10 o'clock last Tuesday, a light appeared in her building that was glorious and otherworldly. Immediately, her and the children had woken up and spoke in other languages, glorifying God. They walked outside in a state of amazement, and they saw that, simultaneously, the other two houses had the exact same experience at the exact same time and were now filtering outside. She continued to explain that from that moment there was dancing, prayer, and singing for an extended time. She said at that point the whole morale of the community dramatically improved. Joy and peace, singing and dancing replaced the sullen despair that had previously clung to their community.

As she was talking to me, I could see over a shoulder there was a group of 20 kids playing in a small field. They looked very ordinary and didn't seem to possess any super-spiritual characteristics. They all wore very dirty, tattered clothes, and most were without shoes. They did, however, seem unusually happy.

I pressed her to repeat the story again, and she graciously did, but she could sense my unbelief and incredulity. At that moment, she put her hand on mine and said, "Don't worry—you'll see. He comes each night now at 7 PM." I was shocked. She had to tell me several times to make sure I understood that at 7 PM Jesus would come to be with them.

We all had dinner together that nigh at 5 PM. We had enough food, and it was more nutritious in variety than the meager staple of corn flour porridge we had earlier. At 6 PM, as the sun began to set, the children finished some chores and went back to their rooms to get ready for an evening gathering. I went to my small hut and tried to imagine what would happen at 7 PM. Mama Grace was so convincing and sincere, I was sure that something remarkable was going to take place.

At 6:45 PM, I walked to the largest of the metal buildings used for classrooms during the day and entered through the doors. There was a dirt floor and no electricity, so a gas lantern was hung from a nail in the ceiling to provide light. Benches were moved to the edges of the room to make an open space in the middle of the room large enough for all the children to assemble.

The children were beginning to sing and dance spontaneously. The songs were more of a call and response style of cadence. Many children had small pieces of tin or sticks or bottles used for percussion instruments. It occurred to me they had never been taught "Christian songs" so they made them up on their own. They were joyous and energetic.

After ten minutes, the music, the atmosphere, and the singing and dancing was so amazing, I thought this must be what Mama Grace meant when she said that "Jesus would come by His spirit at 7 PM." However, it was 6:55 when I looked at my watch; we still had five minutes to go.

At exactly 7 PM, several things happened simultaneously that were astonishing and honestly somewhat frightening. I was the only person in the room wearing a watch, and I kept close track of the time. All of the children either had their eyes closed in prayer, were dancing, or singing. All at once at 7 PM, there was a sensation that the physical atmosphere in the room changed; it's hard to describe. It was not so much like wind, but like all of the air was taken out of the room and immediately replaced with different air that had a different tangible content. The singing and dancing turned quickly to hushed prayer, weeping, and voices of thanksgiving. The children's voices grew louder and the prayer tuned to travail. I can't say exactly what else happened, because I found myself kneeling face down on the dirt floor almost involuntarily. I won't share my private prayers or thoughts that happened during this experience—they are too personal. I will say the feeling that most gripped me was the strong desire for God not to come any closer to me so I would not suddenly perish, though there was also an overwhelming sense of peace, thankfulness, and repentance.

NEGATIVE SPIRITUAL FORCES

I want to say a brief word about negative spiritual forces. I don't like to dwell on such things, but they are a reality. Without the view that negative spiritual forces exist, we place the blame for effects in our own life and those around us wrongly. We all can be influenced by malevolent spiritual forces. Our beings have a spiritual component that is vital and capacious. Negative spiritual influences work together to distract and defeat individuals from true fulfilment and true spiritual reality. If you find interaction with certain individuals or visiting certain places or having exposure to certain media produces unwholesome, anxious, or fearful reactions, consider taking action to eliminate this exposure.

INTERNAL NEGATIVE VOICES

The internal voice of negative spiritual influence seldom speaks in the third person. Not often does it say, "Dave, you're no good, you're a failure, no one loves you, you should stop your pursuits now before things go wrong." No, in a much more subtle, malicious, and sadistic manner, the voice is disguised to sound like your voice. You will think, "*I* am no good, *I* am a failure, no one loves *me*, *I* should stop *my* pursuits now before things go wrong, *I* am a failure and should give up now."

I find there are two main misconceptions that come from negative spiritual influence. The first tries to get you to focus on every bad, negative aspect of your life continually, to produce constant thoughts of failure, guilt, and regret. The second asserts that God is angry with you and wants to punish you or God is too distant and can't be appeased. Because of this, it is imperative to develop the Spirit Circle of the 3C Strategy, using the information in the *3C Companion Guide*. It will bring truth and clarity and begin to silence any negative spiritual voices.

3C EXERCISE

This is the foundational 3C Exercise for the entirety of this material. As I stated earlier, the preeminence of the Spirit Circle cannot be overstated. This is perhaps the most intimate and personal section to address. As I have been somewhat vulnerable and transparent in my writing, I am asking for some additional trust. Please take the time to read, reflect on, and answer the questions below. Seriously consider obtaining my free *Spiritual Life Application Guide* at Dave Yarnes.com.

- Have you personally experienced the grace of God?

- Have you experienced conversion by receiving the grace of God by believing in the birth, death, and resurrection of Jesus Christ and praying a prayer like the one I prayed in the chapter above?

"God, I want you in my life. I feel lost and far away. Please come and take control of my life. I believe the death of Jesus, Your Son, paid for my sins and my entry to commune with You in my life. I want to experience the grace that Dave writes about. I pray in Jesus' name."

- If you have been a long-time follower of Christ, what are the areas of your spiritual life that are most in need of improvement?
  - Prayer?
  - Giving?
  - Meditation?

- If you are from a faith other than Christianity, what has been your predominate view of personal spirituality?

- Have you identified your spiritual strengths? What are they?

- What does continual growth in the Spirit Circle look like to you?

- Develop a spiritual action plan for your life:
  - Active Meditation
  - Reading spiritually nourishing and uplifting resources
  - Talking with God/Prayer
  - Listening for the voice and direction of God
  - Spending time with like-minded believers

NOTES

1. All historical information concerning Alcoholics Anonymous is from http://www.aa.org/pages/en_US/historical-data-the-birth-of-aa-and-its-growth-in-the-uscanada.

2. AA Steps modeled from information on www.recovery.org/topics/alcoholics-anonymous-12-step/.

CHAPTER 6

CIRCLE OF SKILLS

"The Lord has filled Bezalel with the
Spirit of God, giving him great wisdom,
ability, and expertise in all kinds of
crafts. He is a master craftsman."
—EXODUS 35:31-32 NLT

As stated earlier, the 3C Strategy is designed to help give focus and actionable steps toward the master topics of Spirit, Skill, and Self-Mastery. This was the simplest breakdown I could find to help individuals build actionable plans in each area. Without this narrowing of focus, the category of life planning was too vast and had too many competing goals. You could make a fourth circle under Self-Development for "physical health and well-being" or an additional circle under the Skill Circle for "Recreation and Hobbies." The key is defining categories, or circles, that overlap but provide for definition of fulfillment within the Circle and the development and implementation of actionable steps.

My understanding for the need for continual overall development in each of the three circles, including the Circle of Skill, came in to clear focus while pursuing one of my most ambitious professional goals. A partner and I had just finished the construction of a new hotel which was part of a major hotel chain. Although I was familiar with being in management in general, I was new to the hotel business and was not familiar with everything involved with managing a hotel. I studied everything I could put my hands on. I worked to learn every detail of the architecture and the construction, but as the opening approached, staffing became one of my biggest challenges. Our job market lacked the surplus of people needed for all the positions. Because of our somewhat remote location, it was also difficult to attract applicants for some of our management positions.

My ambitious goal was to win the coveted Hotel Quality Excellence Award. Not only is this award prestigious in the industry, it's very difficult to achieve. There is peer-to-peer measuring with hotels, and there are continuous customer surveys. The empirical data is scrutinized repeatedly. So I was not just focused on opening a profitable hotel, but also reaching my goal of winning this award. My aim was to hire a staff that would help us achieve this award-winning status.

One night, as I combed over the holes in our personnel plan, I came up with what I thought would be an excellent idea—I had no idea this would turn out to be disastrous. I began soliciting potential applicants from the growing number of pastors, missionaries, and church workers I knew in the area. I thought, "Who better to promote excellence than some of the areas' top spiritual leaders?" I could not have been more wrong.

I began holding interviews, reviewing resumes, and filling our roster with some of the most significant spiritual men and women who lived in our area. As the selection process moved to the training phase, several things began to alarm me. There were a great deal of people showing up late for the meetings. The breaks and lunch hours, although filled with Bible studies and prayer, began to run past their allotted time. The detailed reporting that was necessary to run a quality hotel operation was slipshod at best. When I began to meet with my new hires to review their performance, they were all very sensitive and attentive, but somehow they didn't get the point. We all had to work very hard to achieve our goal.

One night, after reviewing our failing progress, in desperation I sat down and combed through our personnel files and key performance indicators. Almost invariably the men and women that I had chosen solely based on their "spiritual aptitude" were performing poorly. I want to state this clearly—I don't feel they had bad character or were in any manner deceitful or trying to shortchange me in their work. They just, without exception, lacked the needed skill and self-development that was required for their positions. Their skill sets were largely formed around interpersonal interaction, counseling, and public speaking. Their self-development lacked the depth, training, and experience needed to manage and motivate other people on the team. Many of them had been working their entire lives on their own or in groups of two or three. Now they were part of a 60-person, close-knit, high-performance organization.

I knew what I had to do, but it was hard. One by one, I sought replacements. Searching primarily for those who had high skill and secondly for those that possessed team development and management experience. One by one, almost without exception, I let go all of my closest Christian colleagues. The men and women I hired instead were highly skilled professionals who knew how to function as a team, though I knew half of them had never attended a church, and those who did I would not have put behind a pulpit. With this new team, the hotel began working smoothly and really serving with the excellence I was looking for. Our team went on to win the Quality Excellence Award for hotel management two out of the five years that I was active in its management.

EXCELLENCE IN SKILL IN THE SCRIPTURES

The opening quote to this section, *"The Lord has filled Bezalel with the Spirit of God, giving him great wisdom, ability, and expertise in all kinds of crafts. He is a master craftsman"* (Exodus 35:31-32 NLT) is from both the Christian Old Testament and The Hebrew Torah (as stated in the Pentateuch), and I find it extraordinary for many reasons. It is the first instance in both documents where the concept of being filled with "the spirit of God" is mentioned. More significantly, this unusual power was given to enable the head craftsman to have the proper skills for the construction of the Temple of God. For this incredible undertaking, Bezalel needed culmination of all three circles for this major work of construction and design with precious metals and gems. This is an amazing example of how the three circles of Spirit, Skill, and Self-Mastery work together synergistically.

It would seem more appropriate that the first mention of this remarkable infilling of the God's Spirit should be in reference to performing miracles, or extreme missionary sacrifice, or remarkable preaching. Instead, in this ancient text, the Spirit of God fills a worker who has a great task before him, so that he can have the necessary mastery to do his work with excellence. This underscores the importance of interplay between the three circles in the 3C Strategy for a fulfilling life.

As stated earlier, a skill is something that requires training and experience that comes from focused education as well as repetition and practice. Our skills are developed through continual, intensive effort. These skills have both a physical and mental component.

Think of a master carpenter. The final pieces he creates are perfect examples of his workmanship. You could inspect and marvel at how flawlessly and skillfully his finished pieces have come together. If you were able to watch him as he labored, you would notice a quick and deliberate pace. A master carpenter completes tasks much quicker than an apprentice. His expertise grows and is shown through his finished work.

This is the nature of skill development. Through the development of skill in accounting, masonry, or public speaking, etc., our finished projects reflect our expertise.

To gain this expertise in a certain skill, it is often necessary to narrow your scope of concentration. You see this often in the medical community where the complexity of our anatomy requires doctors to narrow their focus and become a specialist in a certain component of medicine.

The powerful combination of training, repetition, and practice, along with an ever-narrowing scope, is what truly develops expertise.

YOUR UNIQUE SKILL SET

There is no rite of passage or ceremony where someone says, "It is now time for you to primarily focus on your individual strengths and skills." I wish there were such a moment.

Initially, your understanding of your unique skills and personal abilities might not be highly defined or even noticeable. However, I guarantee that you will achieve more success in your field and enjoy more of the life that you are destined to live if you can be strongly intentional about identifying and focusing on personal skills with the greatest potential. This focused approach is fundamental to channeling passion and charting a course.

Be intentional about identifying and focusing on personal skills that have the greatest potential

Identifying your individual strengths and skills and the areas where you have the ability to achieve exceptional mastery can be a significant journey. In fact, it will take purposeful, focused effort on your part. There are several reasons for this.

As individuals, we can tend to be self-deprecating. We underestimate our skills, and we think, "If I can do it, anyone can." There is a built-in tendency toward unpretentiousness and believing others are equally as skilled as we are in any given area. Humility can be a virtue, but a continual self-deprecating mindset that devalues our personal strengths is a detriment to our prosperity and success.

There are skills that you possess and operate at a higher level than those around you. As you chart your course to a fulfilling and prosperous life, you will recognize areas of strength among your personal traits and recognize that you have the ability to become extraordinary in these areas. Sometimes it helps if you realize that you are not prideful, but you are accepting the gifts that God gave you. I have used the question "what can you become the best in the world at" in executive coaching exercises.

Many people fail to identify their own areas of extraordinary skill where they have the potential for greatness because they operate in those areas naturally, with little effort, and wonder why others are struggling. They are dumbfounded when someone else can't see it because the solution is so apparent to them or the physical task is so easy for them. This natural ease can cause us to not see our signature strengths or undervalue them because they are so easy.

INTENSE PRACTICE: THE 10,000-HOUR RULE

Malcolm Gladwell in his book *Outliers: The Story of Success* popularized a scientific finding by researchers who discovered that those who become the world's master craftsmen spend a minimum of 10,000 hours in training and practice of their skill. That is the equivalent of ten years of preparation at about 20 hours per week.

Gladwell outlines the stories of the Beatles and Microsoft as examples. In both instances, he argues their world-class success was not due to chance, but development of skills. They identified, honed, and practiced for 10,000 hours the thing they could be best in the world at.

SKILL AND TIME MANAGEMENT

One foundation in fulfilling 10,000 hours of practice needed for mastery as defined by Gladwell is skillful management of your time. For the past 2 years, I have led many seminars and workshops on the topic of time management. Because of the importance of the time necessary to develop true expertise, successful individuals are those who have significant time-mastery skills.

At different levels, we often have too much to do and not enough time to accomplish it. In order to continually develop our skills, we have to make tough choices. Time is inflexible; therefore, we must adapt and employ self-management and discipline if we are to possess expertise in any skill.

High-demand experts have "paid the price" by continually choosing skill-development activities like studying, reading, practicing, and training over other less important activities competing for their time. Simply put, those things of highest value to us must be scheduled in priority to ensure they are accomplished. If this is not the case, those things of lesser importance will fill our schedule and keep us from full development of important areas of life.

"PRACTICE IS THE CAUSE OF ACHIEVEMENT"

Daniel J. Levitin, author of *This Is Your Brain on Music: The Science of a Human Obsession*. Levitin is a neuroscientist and psychology professor at McGill University in Montreal. He wrote that time spent in practicing a skill is the most important factor in determining success. Practice provides a level playing field where people of many backgrounds and talents can achieve greatness.

> In several studies, the very best conservatory students were found to have practiced the most, sometimes twice as much as those who weren't judged as good.... In another study... Several years later, the students who achieved the highest performance ratings were those who had practiced the most, irrespective of which "talent" group they had been assigned to previously. This suggests that practice is the cause of achievement, not merely something correlated with it.[1]

ACCOMPLISHMENT IN THE SKILL CIRCLE

Those who develop their skills in that private world of personal practice gain the ability to be in demand in their field. In every aspect of life, skills can make the difference in how much impact you have on others. When you achieve mastery in a skill set, you are not only highly capable, but also known for being innovative and possessing emotional strength, creativity, and extreme focus.

ROLE OF MENTAL ATTITUDE IN DEVELOPING SKILLS

Two waiters were scheduled to work on the same day at a certain restaurant. When one woke up, familiar thought patterns from childhood filled his mind with resentment of abusive situations from the past, failure in college, and perceived mistreatment by almost everyone, including his current employer. He dressed carelessly for work, and he was not attentive to the patrons he was serving. His untidy clothes and his attitude revealed the inner condition of his interior thoughts.

His coworker awoke with an entirely different mindset. He was full of gratitude as he prepared for work, because he had been studying college courses online and he saw his job as a means to continue his education. As a waiter, he had met some incredible people through interactions on the job. He was intentional about looking for opportunities to learn from those he encountered. These new people had given him critical information that had helped him shape his education and his life plan. Restaurant work was hard, but it helped instill in him a sense of exactitude and excellence that he could transfer to other jobs.

Here's my question. At the end of the night, whose pockets do you think would be filled with tips? I'm sure you'll agree it's the man with the self-empowering thought pattern and lifestyle. He was mentally focused on his life plan and daily taking steps to achieve it.

The first waiter was focused on his problems. He had not matured to the point in life where we mentally switch from focusing on our problems and weaknesses to evaluating and capitalizing on our strengths. For most of us, this takes place subtly and naturally as we move forward into careers, vocations, and avocations.

We all must transition from focusing on our disadvantages, shortcomings, weaknesses, and undeveloped areas to focusing on our strengths and corresponding skill development. It is largely a personal decision and a function of individual intentionality.

THE SKILL OF PROACTIVITY

Taking initiative, coupled with focused action, is at the heart of the needed skill of proactivity. Stephen Covey wrote about pro-

> Taking initiative, coupled with focused action, is at the heart of the needed skill of proactivity.

activity in his book *The 7 Habits of Highly Effective People: Powerful Lessons in Personal Change* in the context of taking responsibility for the direction of your life. This includes not only what you do, but also what you think. A profound change happens when we realize our life is not at the mercy of external variables. Each of us has the ability to choose, even in situations where our choices can be limited; we ultimately have the ability to choose how we view those situations.

Proactivity is self-initiated behavior that results in forward action. It is based on your realization that you are ultimately in charge of what you choose to do or not to do. Actions taken in alignment with your passion cause you to own your life and chart your course. Proactivity is taking control of your life plan and making things happen for your own advancement, rather than waiting for somebody else to make it happen. My observation is that individuals can take years waiting to be discovered while they should have been taking initiative. To say it clearly, only you can help you. This can only be done by taking responsibility for your thoughts and actions and being proactive.

REJECTING NEGATIVE THINKING

Precious time is wasted every day on self-defeating thoughts and blame-filled thinking that could have been employed in skill development. As you embark on significant life changes, you may be battered by negative thoughts, past failures, and the criticism of others. If left unchecked, these thoughts can keep you from the ultimate goal of proactively taking control and responsibility for your life decisions. Rejecting negative thinking is a skill.

Here are examples of negative thoughts that hinder proactivity and progress which should be rejected:

- "She makes me angry."

- "I'm just like my father."

- "It's just not in the cards for me."

- "I'm not old enough."

- "I'm too old."

Proactive thinking—She can't make me angry it's always my choice on how I will respond. It's me. I won't blame others any more. I have seen people realize with a jolt that they have been placing blame on others. This, in turn, relinquishes personal control by ascribing the power of change to others. *"If she would only stop_____, then I could _____."* One of the most freeing realizations comes when we understand that despite the actions of others, I alone have the ability to choose how I will act and respond.

Negative thinking—It's not me. If only you would change. Not wanting to accept responsibility, individuals want to continue placing blame on others. Often, these mental crutches have been in place for so long that to remove them by taking responsibility would mean notable change in their conversation, attitude, and actions.

OVERCOMING OBSTACLES

I have learned that individuals from dismal and dysfunctional backgrounds have a strong, pervasive temptation to hold disempowering views of the future based on their history. Old negative voices and past experiences have a way of projecting themselves into their future.

- "I've always been this way."

- "Nothing works out for me."

- "I'm setting myself up for disappointment. I'm going to quit now."

- "My father always told me I would never amount to anything."

You are not destined to be a product of your past! You have a unique ability and responsibility to place empowering interpretations on your past. Further connecting with God (through the activities outlined in the Spirit Circle) gives you the infinite ability to recreate yourself anew. This process begins with taking proactive control of every mindset in life.

SKILL OF REACTING TO REJECTION

Developing skills is all about repetition and practice. You start a project, and you develop skills over the course of that project. Project-completion is one form of practice that increases your skills, but it can also be a place to practice your reaction to rejection. Learning how to deal with rejection and criticism is a life skill that, when mastered, will help you unlock many others. Let's say an individual is unduly criticized or rejected at their workplace. Fear, defeatism, self-pity, and resignation based on faulty self-talk can develop into disempowering mindsets.

- My ideas are never good enough.

- I never get the recognition I deserve.

- The boss has favorites.

- I'm afraid of losing my job.

Many individuals never take advantage of the opportunity to develop the skill to handle rejection and develop empowering self-talk.

SELF-EMPOWERING DURING TIMES OF SETBACK

Realistically, there will always be criticisms and temporary setbacks as we hone our skills. However, you can choose to view them as challenges. This is a powerful and productive truth.

Do not take too lightly the need to regulate your internal conversations during situations of seeming setback. The difference between ultimate success and failure often lies in your ability to reframe your internal conversation and employ self-empowering thoughts.

We have all seen how two people can have the same experience, yet one of them tells the story with an empowering view of how much she learned and accomplished while the other one tells the same story with despair, anger, and a sense of fatalism.

I have a lifestyle where I'm engaged often in public speaking, sometimes to large audiences. Often, right before stepping up onto the platform to speak, some event or conversation will occur that could cause a stream of debilitating thoughts. Someone might suggest that the conference attendance is low or I might hear a negative comment about another speaker—these potentially negative comments are often amplified by the common anxiety around performing well as a public speaker. I've found that it's necessary for me to sequester myself into an environment, physically or just mentally, where I can take the time to remember and review the hundreds of encouraging comments from people who have benefited from my books and events. It's important to recall why you are doing what you are doing and gain the positive thoughts that will work to empower you.

FULFILLING YOUR POTENTIAL

If you ever get tired of going through life frustrated from fighting lifelong currents that go against your unique gifts leaving them untapped and undefined, you can change.

You may know someone who has had vast training in a field but after talking with them, you discover that something is not lining up between who they are and what they are doing. A nurse is missing the deep compassion and patience necessary for that vocation. A friend you see every day has the potential for greatness but never musters the boldness needed to pursue their dreams.

If you were to take the time to analyze each person's story, you would find that many of these people never embarked on the journey to become congruent with their true selves. Many think it's too late to develop new skill sets aligned with their unique passions. For example, if they are in a hard-driving sales environment, but they have a passion for creativity, they can live in a constant state of frustration.

Imagine that a man or woman loves accounting for every last dollar. This awakens something within them, and they find meaning and purpose in this task. If that person works in an environment that is solely based on human interaction and a zest for people skills, they would probably live a life of frustration.

You are not too old or too advanced in your career or your life to embark on this change in your journey. I have seen transformative times of change, that should have taken years, be fulfilled in a matter of weeks. All it often takes is the courage to start.

Often the smallest of changes and intentional movement toward change to: igniting your passion, charting your course, and owning your life can yield substantial results. In chemistry, if you change one chemical in a chemical compound, you change the entire substance. Likewise, changing one component of your life to become congruent with who you are and what matters most causes a chain reaction that begins to unleash your hidden potential.

You have a unique mandate to fulfill. This journey might seem overwhelming if you looked at all the steps to be accomplished, so focus on the first few.

3C EXERCISE

Develop the 3C Plan and chart your course and own your life by identifying and initiating action. Use the *3C Companion Guide* to record your responses to these topics to maximize and deploy your greatest strengths.

Consider your skills in these areas:

- What skills are unique to you?

- What can you be the best in the world at?

- Can you develop a simple and consistent plan for personal skill development?

- What skills do you see as gifts from God?

- What skills give you a competitive advantage?

- What skills would you enjoy developing?

- What skills and activities are needed to fulfill your life plan?

- What actionable steps can you take in your Skill Circle? Is there a class to take, or a hobby to pursue, or a mentor who can train you? Define and take some actionable steps.

NOTE

1. Daniel J. Levitin, *This Is Your Brain on Music: The Science of a Human Obsession* (Kindle Edition). Publisher: Plume; 1 Reprint edition (August 3, 2006).

CHAPTER 7

CIRCLE OF SELF-MASTERY

"He opened the big box, and Dorothy saw that it was
filled with spectacles of every size and shape. All of
them had green glasses in them. The Guardian of
the Gates found a pair that would just fit Dorothy
and put them over her eyes. There were two golden
bands fastened to them that passed around the
back of her head, where they were locked together
by a little key that was at the end of a chain the
Guardian of the Gates wore around his neck."

—*The Wonderful Wizard of Oz* by
L. FRANK (LYMAN FRANK) BAUM[1]

One iconic moment in motion picture history is the unmasking of the all-powerful, all-knowing Wizard of Oz in front of the cowering quartet of Dorothy, the Tin Man, the Cowardly Lion, and the Scarecrow. As they bow before a flashing image of the Wizard, seeking his help, the façade of the smoke and mirrors is overwhelming until the little dog Toto pulls back the curtain. Suddenly, they discover that it is all an illusion. The "Great Wizard" is actually a feeble old man working his sound system, images, and pulleys from behind a curtain. Oz had created this persona that he wanted others to see, instead of seeing who he really was.

In the original book called *The Wonderful Wizard of Oz* by L. Frank Baum, before Dorothy and the others meet the Wizard, they arrive at the gate of the Emerald City where each one is fitted with a pair of green-tinted glasses before they are allowed to enter. The tinted glasses give every resident and visitor the illusion that the city is built from green emeralds.

PERSONAS AND PERSONAL BIASES

Just like the Wizard of Oz, all of us have a lens we use to view ourselves and our world. This lens can often be distorted. We also, each have a persona of how we would like the world to view us, and often it is not a real depiction of who we are or how we're perceived. We often feel the need to present a better version of ourselves. This persona becomes a way to filter how we interact with the world around us and, at its core, it hinders us from maturing and growing in Self-Mastery.

Also, just like those tinted glasses in Oz, we all go through life with our own tinted view of the world that we have formed from our personal likes and dislikes, propensities, and habits. This process begins during our early years. The distortions from our personal biases and prejudices can become extreme, as in the case of phobias, violent prejudice, hatred, or unsettling fears. They can also be benign and manifested in preferences for jobs, employees, friends, likes and dislikes that each of us possesses.

Progress begins when each of us realizes that all of us have been fitted with a pair of glasses, regardless of education, background, study, and culture. The question is not *if* you will develop colored lenses to view the world, but whether you are willing to admit on a day-to-day basis that you are using them (your personal biases) to make decisions and to form opinions. In self-mastery, it is important that we can let the world see who we truly are and also take a clear undistorted look at individuals and the world around us.

PERSONAL GROWTH IN SELF-MASTERY

When I examine the lives and personalities of prosperous people who have achieved a high level of Spirit, Skills, and Self-Mastery, their self-worth and purpose allow them the freedom to be themselves and to constantly develop in maturity. They have strong character qualities and a commitment to the underlying principles of fulfilment and prosperity.

FOUR LEVELS OF SELF-MASTERY

There are four classic progressive levels of Self-Mastery. These four levels will give you a grid for gauging your current level and path for progress.

Once you can identify where you are and understand areas of needed transformation, you can begin to grow in your unique Self-Mastery Circle.

Self-Mastery Overview

Level 1—Self-Awareness. Like the people of Oz, at first you don't know that you are wearing green glasses and you think that what you see is the only reality. Self-awareness is a mirror stage where you begin to see yourself more accurately. This process takes honest reflection, self-examination, and some courage. You become aware of your green glasses—your private, often inaccurate, interpretation of everything in the world—so that you can begin to see the need to adjust to reality and begin the process of Self-Management.

Level 2—Self-Management. You begin changing the needed areas of your life using focused awareness and by applying personal discipline. You put aside any persona allowing for increased congruency and openness. Self-Management is the lifelong process of true self-identification coupled with practical self-change. You identify things about yourself that need to be improved, and you courageously confront and begin to change them.

Level 3—Empathy. You have made so much progress in Self-Awareness and Self-Mastery that you are now able to consistently look beyond your own needs and tinted vision to understand others. You develop a true desire to recognize others, even with opposing views, without judgment. You develop positive regard, which accepts and supports a person notwithstanding what they say or do. The term is believed to have been coined by the psychologist Carl Rogers.[2] It involves valuing and recognizing the best in people and the world around you. At this level, you are now affirming others and their potential, while engaging in exploration, discovery, and the search for the best in people.

Empathy entails understanding, not necessarily agreement.

You can now work effectively with a team. You may also be entrusted with greater responsibilities under authority. People begin to be drawn to you naturally.

Level 4—Leadership. At this stage, you are an empathetic and objective facilitator of change. You can discern when to help others and when to stand back and let them solve problems, on their own, so that they can grow. You embody the qualities of fairness and inspiration. You have high expectations, but provide encouragement, support, and recognition. As you move beyond your own self-interest, you inspire others to do the same. You can be trusted with high levels of leadership and are considered a statesman in the way you carry yourself.

SELF-MASTERY LEVEL 1— SELF-AWARENESS

Lack of Self-Awareness

It has been my experience that many individuals cause themselves and those around them a great deal of pain and abrasion when they lack Self-Awareness. They are not aware that their view of the world is simply their own personal perspective. There is an overwhelming need to force their views and opinions on others. It's their individual worldview and it has a tinted lens. This view is colored by prejudices, background experiences, education, inner wounding, and cultural perspectives.

When they interact with others, they do not recognize that they have biases, so they are continually confronting people and being confronted themselves. They find it difficult, if not impossible, to see the viewpoints of others or admit when they are wrong. This becomes a never-ending, awkward way of finding their way among those with differing opinions, mindsets, backgrounds, and worldviews.

Their emotional outbursts can continue unbridled. They seldom become aware of the damage caused by escalated emotion.

Without Self-Awareness, you are not aware of your limitations or how you're perceived by the world around you.

Without Self-Awareness, you are not aware of your limitations or how you're perceived by the world around you. You are uninformed and underexposed. You don't know what you don't know.

Before Self-Awareness, you are mostly self-centered and biased, and this is obvious to others. However, through Self-Awareness you become aware that you have not been objective about how you have viewed the affairs of life. You have seen everything your own way. You thought your view was the only infallible view of the world. When you woke up and realized that you were wearing green glasses, you took them off.

Thinking back on people and situations, I'm sure you would be able to more easily identify people who had different levels of success in many arenas, but were defeated in the area of Self-Awareness. They were like bulls in a china shop—trampling on people, their ideas, and their perspectives. They either seem victimized or tyrannical. They were unable to be proactive because they were putting the blame on others around them whom they feel simply "don't get it." Meanwhile, they lack the ability and the skill necessary for Self-Awareness.

Self-Awareness is the foundation of Emotional Intelligence.[3] It is the ability to view yourself interacting in a situation objectively to see how you look to others. It is an important step in the process of Self-Mastery.

Need for Self-Awareness

The need for Self-Awareness is becoming more and more crucial as our planet becomes more globalized. Every day, we find ourselves interacting with people with significantly different cultures, upbringings, backgrounds, religions, ideals, likes, and dislikes.

Cultural biases are perhaps the deepest level where we need to reorient our lenses. Our lenses have been crafted at a young age with literally thousands of cultural preferences of which most of us remain unaware. Cultural differences are so pervasive that we receive impressions from parents, teachers, co-workers, television, films, billboards, advertising, and other means in both overt and covert ways.

In the early stages of building Self-Awareness, there may be a somewhat negative connotation to the process because you are being awakened to a true view of self with all of your faults as well as your abilities.

Engaging the Right Friends to Advise You

Example Conversation:

I once had a manager that was doing a great job in many areas, but had one large flaw in follow-up. His performance review in other areas was always outstanding, but after our meetings, he seemed to forget major instructions and not complete projects that we had agreed to. This became so critical that after several warnings, I was looking at terminating his employment. Fortunately, I had an accomplished executive coach who was working with me on a seminar the week I was faced with this issue. I asked her if she wouldn't mind sitting in on a meeting with me and the manager that I was considering firing. She agreed, and she sat through the meeting and witnessed our exchange as I went over the projects with the manager. He, again, seemed to have forgotten to follow up with many of the assignments I had tasked him with. I was frustrated and thought it was very obvious that he should be fired, but the executive coach had a different perspective. After the meeting, she was able to give some extremely helpful advice that saved the manager's job and allowed me to keep a great employee. From her previous experience she was able to quickly identify that my manager couldn't distinguish directives when they were given verbally. She told me certain individuals must have directives in writing before they can internalize them and see them as necessary assignments and not just suggestions. After that, I started following up the meetings with that particular manager with a written recap and a list of priorities and assignments; the transformation was extraordinary. My problem manager became one of my most trusted workers, once I understood what he needed to have clear assignments.

I have often used third-party objectivity to aid me in my interactions. This can provide the needed perspective to vastly increase Self-Awareness. Here is an example that you can adopt and use. John says, "Fred, I'm going to take a chance to talk with Bill today about collaborating on some projects. Tell me what you think about this conversation."

Then John begins to role-play a possible conversation as Fred listens. John has taken a step toward Self-Mastery by proactively seeking Fred's third-party objectivity. This will help him to compensate for his own blind spots and the limitations of the lens with which he views the world.

Fred responds, "John, that sounds great, but you might be a little too strident in a couple of areas that Bill might interpret as being overly assertive. I think a few changes in your phraseology will build more consensuses."

John will likely be spared now from a negative reaction by Bill that could have derailed the project.

Open Interaction

The power of taking a few simple steps that open us up to honest communication is a profound advantage in every area of our lives—from interaction with our children to interaction on business or social levels, from public speaking to interpersonal communication. The key is gaining Self-Awareness—the ability to come outside of your personal perspective and view a conversation or setting with third-party objectivity.

SELF-MASTERY LEVEL 2— SELF-MANAGEMENT

Self-Awareness is the Level of Self-Mastery where you learn to see yourself as you truly are, with all your positive and negative tendencies. Self-Management is Level 2 of Self-Mastery where you move from observations about yourself to actively changing yourself.

As an integral part of Self-Management, I have observed that the best sustainable plan for change provides measures that produce more than a temporary quick fix but permanent changes in deeper areas such as perceptions and lifestyles. This deeper, more profound effect occurs only when you take factors of sustainability into account and plan actionable steps. There are three key factors I evaluate when developing a sustainable plan. As you develop your plan for Self-Mastery, be sure you are keeping these three key factors in mind.

1. Consistent Focus on Long-Term Goals

I find that even though many of the executive coaching and self-help programs available can be beneficial, especially for bringing short-term gains, perhaps the reason that they do not produce lasting change is that the methods employed are more like a sprint than a marathon. In contrast, using the values presented in this book, while developing your personal 3C Plan, will help create long-term productivity. Making actionable steps for each Circle will continue to produce an increased harvest year after year.

2. Recognition of Personal Limitations

Sustainability begins with honesty and humility, and true sustainability is built on a holistic approach to the complexities of life.

When we push aside vanity and realize that each of us has limitations, the result is healthy. These limitations can be as simple as the number of hours in the day.

At the point where pride and vanity are broken and we see our limitations more objectively, true enlightenment comes. We realize that for us to live effective, productive lives, we need to learn how to stay focused. We need to monitor our resource levels, provide for a comprehensive long-term view with specific goals and objectives, and come to grips with life's limitations.

3. Ability to Follow an Integrated Plan

Many of us try to compartmentalize work, family, and spirituality into separate, unique categories. Actually a more integrated approach to life, breaking through some of the compartmentalized walls, seems to significantly increase sustainability. Rather than trying to put different aspects of our life into different compartments, it is helpful to operate from an integrated whole that recognizes the value and inter-relatedness of different spheres of life.

To truly create lasting success, your plan needs to be tailor-made for you specifically, with your long-term goals in mind, your personal limitations in consideration, and each part of your life represented. Be honest with yourself as you consider these factors in growing in Self-Awareness.

Self-Management of Emotions

Certain levels of anger, frustration, or anxiety can cause you to lose your objectivity and blind your Self-Awareness. Physiologically, chemicals are released into your bloodstream which further distorts your perspective and aid in serious, long-term health issues.

Try to recognize early signs that your emotions may be becoming problematic before they become chemically enhanced, because once they reach this level, it will take time for your body to dissipate these effects. If you think you may be overreacting, stand up and take a break. It's important for each of us to know our selves well enough that when we are getting into a situation of heightened emotions, we learn how to recognize it and how to take action to compensate.

To be honest and transparent with you, and with a large degree of vulnerability, I want to express some of my personal experiences concerning self-managing emotions. For many of us, our formative years and the environment where we grew up have played a significant role in the development of our interaction with the world. I once heard someone say, "what you are now is where you were when," meaning the person that we have become, the way we interact with the world and our choice of emotional response is a direct product of where we developed and matured—usually between the ages of 4-16.

Although I absolutely believe we are able to change our outlook and response at any time in life, I also believe that there is some pre-programming that needs to be examined as part of growing in Self-Management. If you were brought up in a household where outbursts of anger were common, especially in parents or perceived authority figures, it's easier to justify and model that in your adult life. If you were raised in an environment where a parent or an authority figure would sulk, become sullen, and withdraw in highly emotional situations, you may have a tendency to model this as well.

This understanding of pre-programmed emotional response was one of the most profound life-changing areas of development for me personally. If I can be candid and perhaps a little bit vulnerable, when I started my career, this area was one of the most challenging for me.

Many times after an emotionally charged meeting, I would find myself noticeably upset to a degree that was not proportional to the event. I would carry it home with me and often lose sleep. If I was confronted during this emotionally charged state, my decisions tended to be reactionary. This was a common response I saw modeled for me while growing up. I lived like this for many years until someone began to talk to me about pre-programmed emotional responses and gave me a clear plan of adjustment. Not only was I able to change my behavior, I was able to understand the root of my response so I was able to continuously address the issue if it came up.

I made a significant step toward change during a high-level international meeting with some of the most high-net-worth, high-impact people I knew. We were in a series of meetings at a hotel near Washington where many had flown in from around the world. We had been working on business structures for some significant not-for-profit organizations and NGOs for two days. Because of the pressing nature of the work we were doing, and the difficulties in scheduling and travel for many attendees, we had "sequestered" ourselves for ten hours a day in a hotel ballroom to keep our focus on getting the work done. Tensions grew over the two days, as is often the case in stressed and closed environments like this one was.

At one point in time, I was extremely aggravated by a committee member who was reporting information that I knew to be completely inaccurate. My first and immediate response was extremely inappropriate. Instead of calmly convincing the rest of the committee of the inaccuracy, my emotions heightened and I began to verbally attack and undermine my colleague. My comments were so forceful and heated that the chairman of the committee immediately called a recess to calm things down. Out in the hall as I talked with the chairman, he could see that I was still emotionally charged. It was then that he gave me some of the most significant insight in my life. He said, "Dave, what we all love about you is your passion. We couldn't be doing half the stuff we're doing without your passion and aggression, especially in the field in Africa. But the last 15 minutes you lost sight of how you looked to others in that situation." Then he added this phrase: "Keep your passion—never lose it. But always maintain your composure and perspective." As I pressed him for clarity, he said, "If you could have been a third-party objective observer, you would've seen what others saw in that moment. You went from being an articulate, intelligent participant to someone aggressively and uncontrollably trying to verbally defeat another individual."

This conversation might not seem significant to you, but this began a process of maturity that would last for over 20 years. Much of the material contained here about Emotional Intelligence and practical application steps comes from the research that I did after this incident.

To a large degree for all of us, if we're not actively engaged in understanding our emotional output, we can make two serious mistakes. The first is to be so emotionally charged that we lose our perspective and our ability to see the situation clearly and objectively. The second can be equally damaging when we become emotionally disengaged, becoming distant and sullen. When you work through this section in the *3C Companion Guide,* work through the exercises carefully and thoughtfully. I can personally attest to the significant role these exercises have played in increasing my effectiveness and fulfillment.

SELF-MASTERY LEVEL 3— EMPATHY

Living a life of empathy opens the door to vast and profound levels of interpersonal interaction. Empathy is not sympathy. Sympathy is a sense of emotional pity for a person who has a different view, situation, or station in life. You give sympathy based on a value judgment of another person's life. You feel sorry for them, mostly because they are not like you.

Empathy is uniquely different in that it employs the art of understanding. To be empathic is to probe more deeply into a situation, trying to understand an individual's unique perspective. When you are empathetic, you try to look though another person's eyes and take on their viewpoint without judging. In short, you walk in their shoes and use their lenses to view a situation from their perspective.

My Experience with Empathy

Allow me to share a true experience that highlights my growth concerning the topic of empathy. During a very busy time in my life, I was simultaneously pastoring a growing church while pursuing several business ventures, including building what would become an award-winning hotel. Time management was extremely important as I struggled to balance all these responsibilities with the priorities of my growing family made up of my wife Gina and our three small boys.

On one particular evening, I was tired and feeling overwhelmed as I drove the one-hour commute home from the hotel construction site. All I could think about was playing with the boys and heading to bed early. When I flipped open my planner on the car seat next to me, I looked down and saw that I had planned a barbecue at my house that evening with some new church members from an outreach event that had taken place recently. Honestly, my frustration and exasperation increased instantly. I realized the event had been scheduled for many weeks and was going to be in my home, which meant that I couldn't leave early. Somehow I had not noticed the scheduled event earlier and now there was no way to cancel.

On the drive home, my attitude worsened. I decided I would try to avoid any conversations or contact with people and just attend the grill. I was so fatigued from decision-making and conversing with clients and vendors all day long, I felt wiped out. The evening went as I thought it would, with about 25 people coming to our event. I took up my position on the back porch, tending the grill and trying to avoid conversation as much as possible. The guests stayed for hours, filtering out in small groups until around 9 o'clock that evening. At that time, I noticed a young couple standing on the back porch, waiting to talk with me.

I was frustrated but realized I was cornered. I recognize the girl was a new visitor to our church who had recently given her life to Christ in one of our home group meetings. As she approached me, she said, "Pastor, I want you to meet a friend of mine, Russ. He really needs some help." Over the next ten minutes, the couple explained to me that Russ, who appeared to be in his mid-20s, was living under one of the bridges nearby. He had also recently kicked an alcohol and drug habit. Now sober for a few weeks, he was looking to turn his life around. Typically, I would be more gracious and empathetic in this type of situation, but honestly, I was feeling the tiredness from the overly long day and I found myself being rough with him. I asked them both pointedly what they expected from me. Russ told me that he had recently gotten a job working for a painting crew, and he would be paid at the end of every week. His plan was to have enough money to rent a room at the local YMCA within the next two weeks of paychecks. What he was looking for was my help to get him a place off the streets tonight so that he could keep his job. He said he knew a place that would rent him a room for $25 a week.

At this point, my frustration increased. I realized that I couldn't just turn the money over to him and blindly trust that he would use the money correctly. I knew I needed to accompany him and make sure the money went to his lodging, for his benefit and mine. Gruffly, I told him that I would drive him and pay for one week's lodging, and, if he came back next week, I would help him more. He agreed, and I grabbed my key, my irritation was obvious as I pointed him toward my car.

As I drove, I was purposely silent, feeling mentally and physically exhausted. Russ sat silently next to me; I knew my frustration was obvious, and he could sense my negative attitude, though he didn't mention it. Halfway through our ten-minute drive, an overwhelming sense of what I perceived to be God's presence filled the car. Immediately I realized I had not even spoken to him about the reality of the saving grace of Jesus Christ. I pulled the car to the side of the road and gave him one of the shortest most frustrated gospel invitations you could imagine. Basically I said, "Your life now is a very difficult, living hell. You've been reaping a lifestyle from some of the decisions you have made. Worse than that, there is a God who loves you and wants to put your life back together and you haven't responded." I can't imagine a more terrible presentation of the gospel. But somehow it pierced his heart. With a sincere, brokenhearted response, he said to me, "Pastor, will you help me find God?" I then spent several minutes praying with him to ask Christ to be his Savior, giving him one of the Bibles and discipleship guides that I carried in my car. I watched him transform right before my eyes. If you've never witnessed this before, it's like watching a butterfly emerge from a cocoon. I could tell that his very being had come to life. We continued our journey, and I thought the highlight of the night was over, but nothing could have prepared me for what happened next.

He guided me through an old industrial neighborhood to the hotel that he had found, and I soon realized it was in one of the darkest, most dangerous neighborhoods of the city. We arrived at a five-story building that looked like it had been condemned years ago. On the first floor, there was a bar and restaurant that was filthy and dimly lit. The building had once been covered in siding, but it was now mostly broken off and the bare patches were covered with half painted boards. We entered through a back door; the parking lot opened directly into the men's bathroom, so we walked past the stalls and sinks to get into the bar. The smell of stale smoke and alcohol was overwhelming.

As we approached the bar, I remember immediately seeing two people who were asleep, head in hands on the bar, and two more that were asleep in a nearby booth. There was a total of ten customers in that bar and half of them were unconscious. The lady tending the bar asked Russ what he wanted. She looked at me suspiciously. I was the one out of place, still in my business suit and tie. He told her that he would like a room for the week, and she said he needed to talk with the owner.

Deep sorrow and pity filled my heart as I realized that the people passed out in the bar most likely worked at some of the nearby factories in the neighborhood. I internally speculated that they would bring their checks to the bar on payday and receive a small room and a tab for which they could get some unhealthy food and lots of cheap alcohol. Looking around the room, I was overwhelmed by the thought of the waste of human life in that place. I was angry at such a place for existing. They were preying on the people, capitalizing on the fact that there were no other houses or rooms to rent within miles of this burned-out industrial area.

A very large man came out of the back room, holding a stack of one-dollar bills and counting them as he walked toward us. "What do you want," he barked. When Russ explained the situation, the boss wrote something on a small slip of paper, reached for a key under the bar, and said, "that'll be 28 bucks, 25 for the room and three-dollar deposit for the key."

Russ turned to look at me, and at that moment, I realized I had forgotten to bring my wallet and had no cash on me. As I felt around the pockets of my suit, I found I did have a checkbook from a business account in my inside pocket. I quietly asked Russ if he would accept a check. I was not sure that they would. The proprietor looked at me pointedly and barked back, "Who is this guy? Is he your parole officer or something?" He reached out his hand to take my check as he looked me over.

Russ looked at me sheepishly and looked back at the owner and said, "No...I guess he is my pastor." I remember this part like it happened yesterday—the proprietor put the bills that he was counting away, wiped his hands on the towel in front of him, stretched out his hand to shake mine and said, "Pastor, thanks for bringing this guy here. I'll personally try to help him." The woman and the man, who I thought were passed out on the bar next to me, seemed to wake up simultaneously. The woman grabbed my hand and looked into my eyes as she said, "Pastor, thank you for coming here. We're glad that you stopped by." The man said the same thing, and asked me if he could come to my church sometime. Within just a few seconds, the rest of the patrons were standing around, thanking me for coming and helping this young boy. They all began wishing me well and asking how they could come to a church service. I was dumbfounded as they kept coming up to thank me. For the next ten minutes, I shook hands and greeted them.

My previous perceptions of the place and the people there smashed and a new picture came into view. These workers were marginalized economically and geographically—there was no other place for them to go. Most of them didn't own a car. This was the only room and board available and affordable. They didn't seem intoxicated. They seem trapped. Many of them worked double shifts and fell asleep in the bar watching TV or listening to music. There was no one to impress there, so they didn't mind napping in the bar and they didn't care how disheveled they looked. Often they had only a short time of rest before they had to walk back to one of the nearby factories to go to work. If they had been drinking that night, it wasn't much. It seemed like a group of desperate people who were very thankful to have someone like me visit their part of the world. It was a place that few people cared to acknowledge was there.

After our time of greeting and well wishing, I worked my way upstairs to help find Russ's new room. The halls were narrow, dimly lit, and often dead-ended abruptly. It seemed like a maze. We had to retrace our steps to try to find the stairwell to the next floor more than once. When we finally got to Russ's room on the third floor, we found a small room with a dingy mattress that was unmade—there were clean sheets and a pillow case laid out on a nightstand beside a chipped glass basin that must have been for water. When I entered, my first thought was that this was one of the most depressing rooms I'd ever seen. But from behind me, I heard Russ say, "Wow, this is nice." I realized there must have been a stark contrast between where he had been living, under a bridge, and his new room.

I spent a few more minutes with him, giving him some instruction with his new Bible. I prayed with him one more time, and then I left him. I turned down the hallway I thought lead back to the stairs, but I hit a dead end. I went back-and-forth down the hallways, trying to find the exit. I went from one floor to the next for the next 20 minutes, but I just couldn't seem to find my way out. I realized that this was a divine set-up. I finally stopped in the middle of the hall, exhausted, frustrated, and quite a bit ashamed of how poorly my attitude had been that evening, and thankful for how rich the experience had turned out to be. I sheepishly lifted my eyes and voice to heaven and said, "God, what are you trying to say to me?" God responded. There was no audible voice, but a very profound and clear message—"Will you help Me pastor the people in all of these rooms you are passing by?" I knew that people all over the world lived in a dark limbo world, just like these people, and I could feel that God was calling me to reach out to them, wherever they were.

I was shocked. My immediate thought was, "Please Lord, not me. I'm building a hotel. I have a young family." But I knew the message was genuine. Could I see past my prejudicial paradigm and realize the significance of human lives that were broken, wasting away, and needing help? From that moment on, my paradigm changed. My preconceived notions about people and their status in life shifted dramatically. God brought new life to the scripture, *"Live together in peace with each other. Don't be proud, but be willing to be friends with people who are not important to others"* (Rom. 12:16 ERV). I began to see past exteriors to the hearts of the individuals. I visited that broken hotel many times, and I've moved on to other locations that have similar desperate people who God cares about—even as I've visited other countries, God has reminded me that people everywhere need a friend to reach out to them and see them as important.

Impact of Empathy

This one experience opened my mind and heart to true empathy—I have become known for reaching people with varying economic and social statuses all over the world. I pioneered poverty relief efforts in Kenya and Uganda, I established Micro Businesses in Peru, and revolving loan funds in India and East Africa. All of these initiatives started with this first encounter with some forgotten people in a dilapidated hotel.

An empathetic mindset can produce some of life's most positive, transformative experiences, especially when others are diametrically opposed to you at first.

Empathy touches a basic human need in others to feel understood and valued. It is difficult, if not impossible, to move on to higher levels of engagement with someone unless that individual feels respected. An empathetic mindset can produce some of life's most positive, transformative experiences, especially when others are diametrically opposed to you at first. You're able to see interactions change as others sense your nonjudgmental desire to understand them.

Surprised by Empathy

Some time ago, I was scheduled for an appointment with a banking executive at my office, but while he was waiting for me I became tied up in traffic. While the staff of our pharmaceutical and hotel accounting office tried to cover for me, he noticed on my desk boxes of literature about our humanitarian response to a recent famine in East Africa. He began to read the literature that described the crisis of recently orphaned children and our relief efforts that were underway among companies I had started.

Most individuals feel sorry for and are sympathetic to this type of story, but sympathy can cause short superficial reaction. For the banking executive that read through this material while waiting for me to arrive, he was moved to empathy from the stories he was reading. By the time I made it to the office, the executive had tears in his eyes and his personal checkbook in hand. He became a most unlikely but most welcome corporate donor. As a by-product, our relationship changed. He saw me and my corporate endeavors from a new perspective. From that point on, we became friends.

Religion and Empathy

Many religious individuals find empathy difficult. In my experience, religious leaders can lack this needed skill because their desire to make their views known is so pronounced that they have difficulty allowing others enough mental space to feel accepted and valued. This happens more frequently if the individuals have dramatically opposing views to their religious beliefs. The religious leader can feel that they are condoning others behavior and lifestyle if they were to ask questions to gain clarity.

For example, imagine there is a young evangelical pastor named Joe who becomes aware of a homosexual couple in his congregation and asks to meet with them privately. Joe starts out the conversation by ardently stating the sinfulness of their behavior. The couple leaves his office and never returns to church again. The posture toward condemning the sin first removed all the potential for an empathetic approach. On the other hand, Joe could have begun with unconditional positive regard by stating that he was thankful they agreed to meet with him and how much he had appreciated their participation. Next he could have engaged in positive inquiry by asking questions: "I haven't had any experience with a homosexual couple in our congregation before. Can you tell me how you view your relationship in light of our Christian values?" This approach will develop a more productive conversation, but Joe, in his insecurity, may feel he is condoning and approving of their lifestyle. If the couple were to have stated a belief opposed to Joe's, he could have courageously responded, "Thanks for sharing this with me. I know it takes courage. Now, I want to let you know why I respectfully disagree." Again, empathy doesn't involve agreement as much as it entails the artful ability to try to understand the other person's perspective. Only after you have the opportunity to consider life from another's perspective should you interject your perspective.

SELF-MASTERY LEVEL 4— LEADERSHIP

The fourth level of Self-Mastery is Leadership or managing others. This can be family leadership, corporate leadership, or community leadership. Whatever type of leadership, it builds from our developed place of Self-Awareness, Self-Mastery, and Empathy. Once you can understand and manage yourself and empathize or understand others' viewpoints, then you can begin to effectively compel and lead others to action. You become a facilitator of change.

There are volumes written on leadership, its components, and practices, but for our purposes we will contain our view of leadership in light of advanced Self-Mastery. Some of you reading this might say that you are not in a position of leadership. I would argue each of us have leadership roles. You may be a homemaker, or a father, or involved in a civic organization; I assure you, there are those around you who you can impact through leadership.

> Once you can understand and manage yourself and empathize or understand others' viewpoints, then you can begin to effectively compel and lead others to action.

Leadership is the result of a lifelong endeavor that begins with self-evaluation, empathy, and the realization that each person's unique perspectives are just that—uniquely individual. At the heart of this approach is setting an example that inspires others to follow. Without this, many unconsciously say "do as I say, not as I do." This is especially evident when we attempt to lead those closest to us, family, friends, and others with personal relationship. At this level, without Self-Awareness and Self-Management, others can spot hypocrisy and incongruence between what we teach and how we live. How many parents have felt this sting as children model their actions more than obey their directives?

Help Yourself First

Recently, while I was traveling on a plane, the stewardess said, "If you are traveling with a child or someone who needs assistance, put on your oxygen mask first so that you will be able to help others around you." It occurred to me that this principle applies to many facets of life. It is important for us to engage in personal self-development and self-mastery so that we will be able to contribute on an ongoing, significant basis to the world around us.

I am reminded of a true story about four men swimming in a river. Two were swimming on the left side of the river and two were swimming on the right. Suddenly, one of the men on the left side began floundering and was about to drown. Fortunately the friend nearest to him was an expert swimmer.

The two on the right side began to call out frantically for to him to save their friend, but the expert swimmer seemed to freeze as he watched the drowning man struggle more and more.

The cries for help increased from the right side of the river. "Help him! Help him!" they shouted, but the one man who was within proximity to rescue him stayed motionless. This went on for what seemed like an eternity.

Finally, the drowning man stopped struggling. He began to take on water and go down. The situation looked hopeless.

At that point, the expert swimmer swam over, pulled him to shore, and began to resuscitate him. An emergency crew came and took him to the hospital. After their friend was on his way to recovery at the hospital, the two friends on the right side of the river began to chastise their companion.

"How could you have been so cruel and let him suffer so much? You could have saved him all this pain if you had thought a little less of your own personal safety."

After their tirade continued for a few minutes, they soon realized that this man knew more than they did. He responded, "I've been a swimmer all my life, and I've seen this happen a number of times. If I had reached him even one moment earlier, he would have clutched on to me with all his strength. With the current being as strong as it is, both us would have lost our lives. As painful as it was for me to watch him struggle, I had to wait until he had completely exhausted all of his own strength and was able to be helped before I could save him."

High Level Leadership

That is an example of Leadership. As a high-level leader, you are able to see the big picture of the crisis, and you are able to restrain your impulse to "jump in" to rescue a situation. You understand the need to sustain your own long-term mental health. If you survive, you will not only help one drowning person, but also live to assist others.

While it is true that the drowning man was in a dire situation and unable to help himself, it is also true that his ultimate survival depended on the mature judgment of the man responding to him.

Many gifted individuals are suffering and not achieving their maximum potential because they are continually responding to the needs of others in an unhealthy way. This can produce an outward veneer of compassion, duty, and responsibility. However, good leaders will take time to consider the whole situation. They will carefully evaluate the resources available and consider their condition and their ability to respond in a way that will produce the best long-term effectiveness for both themselves and those around them.

It is true that we gain significance by helping others. However, when we take time to evaluate our additional financial, mental, and physical resources, our capacity to aid others grows exponentially.

Know When to Lead

Imagine that Jerry walks into his supervisor Mary's office and Mary says, "Jerry, we have a department that has been nothing but problems. Production is almost non-existent. There is constant quarreling and morale is at an all-time low. Based on your stellar record, Jerry, we would like to make you responsible for this department and its success. However, if it continues to fail, you will be let go."

At this point Jerry could jump in blindly and take this leadership responsibility, with the hopes of becoming a hero to the company. But being a little wiser, he asks questions about his authority. "What type of decision-making authority do I have to make changes?"

Mary answers, "The workers are all family members of the CEO and can't be touched. Also, we have no money or time for any retooling, either managerially or with the equipment. You won't be able to interface with the suppliers, the customers, other departments, or other supervisors. Now do you want the job or not?"

This sounds preposterous. We can agree that Jerry would be making a terrible mistake to take on this area of leadership without the authority to make changes. Yet often in real life we try to take leadership and responsibility in situations that we actually do not have authority to change.

It is important to be sure you are only taking leadership and responsibility over situations that you *do* have authority to change. However, what about situations that are more subtle in nature, such as trying to change your spouse? All of us who have been in long-term relationships realize that there is always personal sovereignty and choice involved and that making changes is based on agreement and relationship. Or what about being responsible for someone with destructive tendencies? The same principle applies. Is there a capacity and a desire for change on their part? The root of dysfunctional co-dependency can often come back to this very issue of taking an unnecessary view of authority and responsibility for trying to change someone else.

If you are in a workplace environment where you do have the ultimate responsibility for what happens, ask yourself if you have been given the corresponding control or authority. Assess what leadership is necessary based on these two components: responsibility and authority.

 # 3C EXERCISE

- Many times in the past, after an emotionally charged meeting, I would find myself noticeably upset, and I would carry it home with me and often lose sleep. Have you experienced similar occurrences?

- What steps can you take to eliminate the "root" thoughts before they become too ingrained?

- When confronted during this emotionally charged state, do your decisions tend to be reactionary?

- Have you been able to recognize your own personal biases?

- How does this aid you in your personal growth in Self-Mastery?

- In varying degrees within different aspects of our lives, we can be at diverse stages of the Four Levels of Self-Mastery. Honestly take time to assess your competence in the following areas:
  - Level 1—Self-Awareness
  - Level 2—Self-Management
  - Level 3—Empathy
  - Level 4—Leadership

- How can you employ the strategy "Help Yourself First" as it applies to life?

- Are you open or closed to correction? Engage in a conversation where you need to grow in this skill.

- Are you open or closed to coaching? What would it take to grow in this area?

The *3C Companion Guide* has expanded and corresponding questions designed to give you further thought and application. Take time to review and reformat the answers from your previous 3C Exercises so that they provide a reference for actionable steps. Perhaps some steps will cover multiple areas of needed growth.

NOTES

1. L. Frank (Lyman Frank) Baum, *The Wonderful Wizard of Oz*. Chicago: April, 1900 (Kindle Edition in the Public Domain).

2. Carl Rogers, *A Way of Being* (1900).

3. See also chapter 3, "Before we Begin, Emotional Alignment."

CHAPTER 8

KEYS TO MAINTAINING A FULFILLING AND PROSPEROUS FUTURE

"You can chain me, you can torture me,
you can even destroy this body, but
you will never imprison my mind."
—MAHATMA GANDHI

The last section of this book is vital and devoted to practical application and keys to deploying your personal 3C Strategy to ignite your passion, chart your course, and own your life. This entails developing a sustainable 3C root system. What does it mean to be rooted and grounded in a "core system" that is empowering and promoting a fulfilling successful life? This occurs when your deepest underlying beliefs are supporting you and nourishing you—your beliefs help you with every step toward fulfilment and prosperity. When you are firmly rooted in a positive 3C belief system, your default mindset is one that continuously supports your progress.

Roots represent that place in your life that others can't see. They contain intentional times alone when we self-examine and strengthen our core beliefs, dreams, and attitudes. Just as roots dig into the soil for both nourishment and supportive strength, the time we spend envisioning and planning our fulfilling and prosperous life provide the mental and emotional foundation "roots" we need. Someone once said, "the fruit we see is the result of roots we cannot."

CORE VALUES

You will need to identify both your current core values as well as those you must develop in order to see lasting change occur in your life. In my experience, uncovering these core values is one of the most significant and profound journeys of discovery a person can take in their lifetime. A person cannot find true direction without knowing their core values. Core values are like the operating system of a computer that allows other applications to run smoothly.

In 2008, I embarked on a journey to form a high-performance New York-based hedge fund. Having already owned and developed a nationally chartered US Bank, I was aware of the necessity of the foundational legal work and preparation involved. I hired one of the state's most experienced attorney groups to help me. The process took months. We had to iron out our strategy and go through the legalities of operating a hedge fund.

> A person cannot find true direction without knowing their core values.

Next we had to draw up the necessary agreements to involve customers and other participants.

At the same time we were developing this legal work, I was going through a time of personal, deep reflection on an investor's responsibility to be socially and spiritually minded. I had watched many of my friends become wealthy, investing in stocks and companies that I felt were antagonistic to my faith. For me, some of the areas of gambling, alcohol distribution, and tobacco sales were problematic. There were also a number of companies that supported a liberal agenda. It was impossible for me to reconcile in my mind being a financial backer of these sectors. For modern investors, there are many groups that specialize in sorting through investments to find opportunities that reflect their client's personal conviction. But in 2006, that wasn't the case.

As our legal team put the necessary corporate charters and documents in place, I worked on developing a code of conduct and core values in a series of socially responsible statements that would guide our trading platform. When I finally finished and presented it to our attorney group, the response was pure bewilderment.

They cautioned me about the serious constraint my code of conduct would put on our ability to make a profit. They advised me to make these decisions internally without having them written into an official corporate document.

The tension between us grew as we approached our deadline for having our documentation and strategy in place. Finally, one evening the showdown came as we worked late into the night. After trying to convince and coerce me into compromising my stance, I simply looked across the boardroom table and said, "You may not understand my core purpose and core values, and I'm not expecting you to. I've heard your considerations and concerns about how this can restrict our fund in the future. Having weighed all of this, it's time for me, as the president and majority owner, to make a decision. We will put our core purpose and core values which represent my Christian faith into all the public documents that we're creating. This will be a guiding star for all of our investors and advisers. In short, these core values are more important to me than pure profit." Our fund launched; the sections of our documentation that clearly stated my Christian values remained intact. Many potential investors welcomed this addition, and others were not as enthusiastic. Most importantly for me, all of our transactions we guided by core values that were deeply important to me.

CELEBRATE SUCCESS AND FORGET FAILURE

Remembering the triumphant and victorious times help to drive core values deeper into the culture of an organization. Celebrating triumphs, while remembering core values and purposes, creates a deep-rooted imprint.

As I mentioned earlier, over the years I have gained significant personal empowerment through continuing to commemorate times of great success such as the opening of a new business or closing large deals. Life comes at you fast. It is important to stop and take time to focus on the victories, because they provide fuel and positive reinforcement for future adventures. Another helpful practice is to look back through the trail of your lifetime to review the "signposts" where you have had times of success.

I have met numerous individuals throughout the years who have led successful lives, but when you speak to them individually, the only things they seem to remember are their failures, struggles, and obstacles. When you take time to commemorate your successes and the success of your team, you demonstrate and reinforce the core values that you want to keep developing.

3C EXERCISE

In the beginning of this chapter, we discussed keys to maintaining a fulfilling and prosperous future. All of us have a history of starting something important and then, at times, neglecting it, procrastinating, or getting distracted. How can we integrate this material into a plan that will accompany us for the rest of our lives?

When we talk about "a sustainable 3C root system" we mean empowering and promoting our deepest underlying beliefs. Take the time to write out your 3C root system. It could look like:

- "I will never compromise my faith."

- "I will always put my family first."

- "I will never get involved in a business solely for the money."

- "I'll never put possessions above people."

These will become true sustainable roots for the rest of your life.

- Often there are core values we grow into that we need to develop to have lasting change. Can you list a few of your core values?

- My core values were challenged significantly as I developed a hedge fund. Have your values been confronted or challenged?

- What has your experience been when you've been challenged?

- Take the time and think through some "non-negotia-bles" and how you will address future challenges.

- When many successful people look back over their lives, they remember failures and struggles. Commemorating and celebrating victories are important for reinforc-ing your core values. Consider some key moments in life that were worthy of celebration—if you have not celebrated them, take the time to commemorate those moments.

- Have you celebrated success with your team, family, or organization by deliberately celebrating success that reflects your core values?

CHAPTER 9

SELF-DEFEATING MINDSETS

"Above all the grace and the gifts
that Christ gives to his beloved
is that of overcoming self."

—FRANCIS OF ASSISI

As a young man, I was quite avid about working out in the gym daily, and I even did some boxing while I was in college. After college, I continued to go to one gym regularly where I frequently noticed a group of young men who always stayed together in a close-knit group.

When I saw their tattoos, clothing, and body piercings, my immediate reaction was that they were gang members. This turned out to be partially true. I decided that I wanted to reach out, befriend them, and gain an inroad to understanding their subculture.

At first, they were extremely suspicious and closed to my efforts at friendship. They realized that I did not have the same background as they did, and they thought for sure that my intentions were disingenuous. Over a period of the next few years, significant events happened that would cause me to be thrust into their confidence.

WINNING TRUST

This was in the early days of what would eventually come to be known as full contact or ultimate fighting. These strong young men had a fight club that met twice a week where they would hold bouts of full-contact fighting. Eventually they were evicted from the premises they had been renting because the owner was extremely nervous about their activities and how it affected his liability. Because they knew that I owned several properties in the area, they became more open to speaking with me, and so I began to meet with them as we discussed our common interests in fighting and other sports.

At that time, I owned several large downtown buildings. They were built in the 1920s, so they had sub-basements to handle warehousing and stock that came in off the city streets. These sub-basements had bathrooms and electricity and large open spaces. They had once housed a workforce of stock clerks and maintenance crews, but had long since been vacant—it was a perfect environment for setting up a sparring floor. I decided to strike a deal with these young men to allow them to rebuild one of the large vacant sub-basements and outfit it for full-contact fighting.

I had a few conditions, though.

One: There must be a complete lack of drugs and/or any nefarious behavior while they were in the building. If any crime was committed by them on the property, our deal would no longer be in effect.

Two: We had to agree on a very strict, safe, and supervised way of engaging in full-contact sports. I wanted to be sure the space was used for appropriate fights and that there was nothing overly dangerous.

Three: I wanted to be included in their fights and training. My condition was that they would let me train with them and that they couldn't remove me from the group, regardless of my performance, my beliefs, or my personal background.

And so we agreed.

IMPRESSIVE WORK

It was amazing to see the amount of effort and care that they put into building that fight club. They mobilized in ranks like a well-formed army—cleaning, building new walls and partitions, and painting. They installed new lights, electrical connections, toilets, and other necessities, using their own funds to furnish out the place. As I watched them, I realized with amazement that they had a desire for excellence in their hearts.

Within a month or two, the building was ready for its primary use. By that time, this subculture's club had invested thousands of dollars into the development of a full-contact, ultimate fighting arena. It was amazing to see how the space had changed with their efforts.

However, for all of their organization, skill, and hard work, I began to recognize that they had deeply rooted values that were holding them back. They obviously had a great work ethic, evidenced by the fully functional arena they built by hand, but I noticed a recurring thought as I got to know them more. Almost without exception, there was a deep mistrust of others. Their cynicism, suspicion, and distrust were prevalent during every conversation.

- "No one is going to pull anything over on me."

- "I saw that one coming."

- "Everyone has an angle."

- "She is a fool for being so generous."

- "No one can be fully trusted."

- "It's just a matter of time before someone turns on you."

They had a deep cynicism toward people and life in general. Negativity abounded in their conversations and their evaluations of others. Even if someone came to them with the purest of motives or opportunities, they often rejected help with suspicion and contempt.

They passed up many good opportunities during the time I worked with them because of their self-defeating attitude. If a project or job seemed to be good or beneficial to an individual or to the group, they would insist it was too good to be true, and let it pass them by. I felt like they were unable to truly evaluate a person or situation that presented itself, because they always approached it by looking for something underhanded or misleading. Interestingly, this was a mindset that I recognized from my own life in years past.

MY OWN SELF-DEFEATING ATTITUDE

I well remember my own personal experience concerning overcoming a self-defeating attitude. I owned a large commercial real estate project in New York. At one time, it had been a five-story downtown shopping center with lots of stores and boutiques and around 70 tenants. I was converting the space into large modern offices and commercial centers when I received a huge break. Two of the largest employers in our area were looking to relocate, and they thought my space provided a great location; however, they were unsure if I could provide them with areas large enough for their needs. Everything was going perfectly, but there was one problem. I had one tenant who needed to move to a different space because he was directly in the middle of the area I needed to renovate. He was one of the leases that I had inherited when I purchased the facilities. He did not pay a lot of money for the space and, quite frankly, we never got along that well. This new renovation project would be the key to my success, and I began to look at him as my sole obstacle.

I procrastinated in talking to him directly, but in my mind I had dozens of conversations with him. During my mental conversations with him, he was always stubborn, demanding, and asking for things that I just couldn't provide. All of these imaginary conversations ended at an impasse. Finally, the day came to talk with him in person.

As I went into his office, I found that I was short, discourteous, pointed, and demanding. As you can imagine, he responded in a similar escalating manner. Finally, I threw down my "bottom line" deal. I said, "John, I can relocate you to the fifth floor. Here's what I can provide for your company and your inconvenience. This is all I can do—take it or leave it." Without any consideration, he pushed the papers back across the table to me and told me he wasn't interested in moving. As I left his office, I remember thinking to myself that the meeting went exactly as I had imagined.

Therein was the problem. My negative view of the potential outcome was so overwhelming. That, coupled with my approach, forced my tenant to react in almost a pre-programmed way. If the stakes hadn't been so high, I probably would not have revisited the situation. But it was decision-making time for a new tenant, and this deal could completely transform my financial model. I needed to revisit the conversation with John. This time, I asked an associate of mine to go with me. He had a great background in commercial real estate, and I thought he could "talk some sense" into my tenant and help direct the conversation.

As my associate reviewed my potential contract, he told me he thought I was being way too generous. I explained that this deal was important and it was a small loss compared to the revenue I would be getting. I also reminded him that my tenant had already turned down this "generous" offer. My associate insisted on making some changes that made the contract much less favorable to my tenant. Reluctantly, I agreed.

When we reached my tenant's office, my associate greeted him politely and talked about the benefits of the new businesses that were coming to the building. We walked him down into the rooms that would be his new space if he took the deal. My associate empathized with John's concerns and assured him we could work through any obstacles. Within an hour, my tenant signed the new agreement.

I was astonished. It was a lesser bargain than the one I had presented a week before. I had gotten nowhere and my associate closed the deal in less than an hour. Since that time, I have realized over and over that my perceived negative perception of a circumstance actually becomes a self-fulfilling prophecy. In short, what I believe is what I get.

Now I take significant effort to make sure that during negotiations or conflict resolution with staff that I can visualize a positive outcome that's mutually beneficial. Once this is in place, everything, from my direction of conversation, body language, and overall tone, is completely transformed. This is an initial step to living a life of maintaining a positive attitude.

Are you influenced by a cynical mentality? Have you been influenced by a worldview with ideologies such as:

- Never let anyone take advantage of you.

- Everyone has an angle, and they are always trying to take advantage of you.

- There are not enough resources to go around, so you better get yours first.

- I'll take from you before I go without.

- I am always suspicious of everyone and their motivations.

These thought patterns have been dramatically influential in the formation of the worldview and paradigms of many. If unchecked, they continue to run in the background and hinder us from moving forward to ignite our passion and chart our course to a fulfilling and prosperous life.

You and you alone have the responsibility and the capacity to create an empowering mindset and corresponding internal thought life connected to your 3C Plan. Research suggests successful individuals have been able to develop and maintain a state of high expectation for life.

Over the years of working with hundreds of CEOs and high-net-worth and high-impact individuals, I have come to believe that the concept you are about to learn is a foundational theme in the lives of most of the most prosperous individuals I have met.

> You and you alone have the responsibility and the capacity to create an empowering mindset and corresponding internal thought life connected to your 3C Plan.

PLANNED INNOCENCE

Most of us have been brought up in an environment where we have been trained to spot flaws and errors. We have been trained to look for trouble. Just like the young men in the fight club, this can grow into a dysfunctional worldview.

However, with self-determination and practice, we can constantly refresh our mental attitudes after daily disappointments and return to what I have termed "planned innocence." Even when things go wrong, we can train ourselves to mentally reestablish a mindset of faith in other people and hope in the world around us. It's important, because otherwise we shut ourselves off from possible relationships and opportunities, too busy protecting ourselves to realize that we are missing out on life.

When you are a trusting person, you are able to focus on the good in people, not their faults. A lifetime of *planned innocence* plays out in the lives of people who have gained great impact, significance, and prosperity.

Often there is a balance to be struck. If you consider a range on a continuum, cynicism would be on one side and gullibility would be on the other side. Different situations can require adjusting on this continuum. The intentional practice of *planned innocence* helps you to continuously come back to a state of trust and openness, while still being mindful that we live in an imperfect world.

ENLISTING THE HELP OF OTHERS

A quick note about trusting and informing others concerning your personal goals and progress: Your close relationships and friendships can help or hinder you on your road to accomplishing your goal of a fulfilling and prosperous life. I'm sure you have learned this already, but here is a powerful key that can help.

If there is something you are trying to quit, such as smoking, overeating etc., as a general rule, you should tell all your close relationships. Their continual accountability will be very helpful to keep you in check. "Why are you eating that cake? You said you were on a diet."

If you have aspirations that transcend your present levels of accomplishment, these goals should be shared discreetly and only in close relationships where the other person truly desires to see you succeed. Sadly, jealousy, insecurity, and misunderstanding can often cause people to react negatively or worse impede your progress.

Further, keeping your goals private often supports accomplishment. Your good feelings from sharing your goals may prematurely satisfy you and you stop working. Derek Sivers, founder of CD Baby, believes it is better to keep some goals secret. Our minds sometimes associate fulfillment of goals with the simple step of sharing it with others.

Honestly ask yourself, during challenging times has your internal thought process been one of empowerment or have you noticed cynicism rising? How do you think this affected the outcome of these challenging moments?

When you examine these questions and adjust your responses, you can develop a root system that enables you to consistently chart your course to a fulfilling and prosperous life.

3C EXERCISE

Recognizing and removing a self-defeating attitude is a key to having a fulfilling and prosperous mindset. Often there is a balance to be struck.

- If you consider a range on a continuum, cynicism would be on one side and gullibility would be on the other side What has been your natural tendency on the continuum of cynicism and gullibility?

- With regard to a prosperous mindset, what are your unique keys to maintaining a fulfilling and prosperous future?

- Can your mindset toward others be changed to help you to be more effective?

- Have you been wise in enlisting the help of others as you chart your course?

There can be a temptation to read the above 3C Exercise and others like it without taking the time to reflect and answer the questions. You owe it to yourself to engage with this type of practical application after each chapter. This development of your individualized 3C Plan, along with its constant application in life, is how you ignite your passion, chart your course, and own your life. Trust me—you'll thank me later.

CHAPTER 10

Love Your Life and Learn from Your Setbacks

"Most great people have attained
their greatest success just one step
beyond their greatest failure."
—Napoleon Hill

THE MOST IMPORTANT CONVERSATION OF YOUR LIFE—THE ONE YOU HAVE WITH YOURSELF

Adversity and obstacles will come to all lives at one time or another to varying degrees. Sometimes, obstacles that seem insurmountable block your way. By programming yourself to see them as challenges and stepping-stones to success, you will be able to keep yourself free from the swamp of disillusion, depression, and despair.

Often the simple action of developing a life strategy using the Three Circle approach helps reduce any feeling of being overwhelmed when difficulties come. It's empowering to realize you may be doing well in one or two circles while a challenge exists in another.

> *How we view the process of recovery when we experience temporary setbacks can make the difference between being stuck and enjoying continuous advancement.*

As we discussed earlier, your internal thought life moves at an astounding rate of 600–700 words per minute. It is your job to be rigorous in your effort to control the most important conversation of your life—the one you have with yourself. Begin by simply using different language instead of saying "I have a problem," you could restate it as "I have a personal challenge" or "there are some obstacles to be overcome." Changing your vocabulary creates a significant adjustment in your thought life.

I have come to believe that God has given each of us the power of choice and one important choice is how to view moments of defeat.

Recovery. Throughout history, we can look at extreme cases of individuals who have gone to the depths of ruin and poverty only to recover at their lowest point and become a prolific role model of reaching one's potential. These have become a source of inspiration for those of us who have grown up in environments that did not provide all the opportunities we would have liked. Their lives inspire many who have suffered extreme setbacks and come to their lowest point, being perceived as failures by others. Many of these setbacks were unavoidable.

Avoidance. However, there are also numerous stories of individuals who were able to avoid setbacks by studying the lives of others and learn from them. It's a common story—the dramatic recovery from bankruptcy or overcoming hardships. These are usually inspirational stories, but the less-dramatic story of avoiding bankruptcy often remains unnoticed, but is equally motivating.

Part of the human condition is suffering setbacks. Regardless of the cause, the pain and ripple effect from these setbacks can be absolutely overwhelming unless you decide in advance that you will continue to love your life and you will learn something new from every setback that comes your way. This advanced preparation allows you to dust yourself off and move ahead without missing a stride.

MAKING THE RIGHT CHOICE FOR RECOVERY

At the core of every recovery story is the option to make the right choice out of three possible and opposing thought patterns:

1. This is my fault.

2. This is your fault.

3. This is my opportunity to learn something.

These are not superficial choices. Your choice affects the way you view significant events in your life and determines whether or not you will recover from them and go on to seize your destiny. At its core, the right choice can change and reprogram your heart with a new method of dealing with adversity that is positive and constructive instead of negative and destructive. We will look at the implications of each of these approaches.

1. *This is my fault.* With this attitude, you ascribe a negative meaning to significant challenges and obstacles in your life. You begin to internally recite a defeatist story that empowers overwhelming negativity. The narrative progresses something like this: "It was my fault and that means I am a bad person. I will never be able to do this right."

2. *This is your fault.* With this approach, you heap all the blame on the other person. You exempt yourself from any contribution to the problem and reason like this: "This is all your fault. I will never recover. You just ruined my life."

3. *This is my opportunity to learn something.* In this third option, you turn the defeat into victory. Instead of allowing those negative voices to become part of your internal

vocabulary, you use the experience as fuel for new creativity and reflection.

Every person has the option to allow defeat to become a permanent source of fuel that burns up every potential opportunity. When you are obsessed with "I was wrong," a past defeat can make you so jaded that every time a new adventure arises, you resort to negative-empowered thinking. You say to yourself, "Oh, that opportunity is not for me. I've failed before. I could never do that."

Another disempowering mindset makes you feel that you are the only one who has ever experienced a certain trauma, life experience, or failure. Therefore, you assume that no one understands exactly how deeply and significantly that setback has affected you.

You also have the choice to simply embrace the fact that mistakes, challenges, obstacles, and even apparent failures come to each of us in the course of our lives. If you have failed, you are not alone. Setbacks can become significant, quintessential turning points for those who find within themselves the ability to reprogram their very nature at the crucial time needed in order to bring about ultimate success.

Let's look at an example. Someone might wake up, get ready for work, and when they step outside, they find they've got a flat tire while their car was sitting in the driveway. One type of person would say, "God hates me. I'm already having such a bad day. I'm going to be so late to work that I'm going to get fired."

Another person with the same situation would look at the tire and say, "This is so fortunate that it happened right here where I can get it fixed. I could have been on the highway last night when it was raining and I was with my family! Everyone has a flat tire once in a while. I'm sure my boss will understand. Maybe I'll meet someone at the repair shop today who will be a good contact for me."

It's the same event—the same flat tire but the response can be completely different.

THIRD-PARTY PERSPECTIVE

In the midst of negative social interactions, such as an argument with relatives or a workplace confrontation, if you take offense at others' words and lay the blame on them, you will be on your way to a negative conclusion. However, if you choose to look at the situation more objectively, you can say, "This is my opportunity to learn something."

What if you had a third party involved in the situation who was able to give you objective observations? This person could make a difference by giving you a fresh viewpoint.

Let's imagine that Andy has a confrontation in the company break room with Reggie, and the conversation escalates into an argument. Nothing is resolved and both men leave the area frustrated. As a result, their relationship is damaged.

Andy is convinced that he is right and Reggie is wrong and there is no middle ground. Without a change of attitude in the future, Andy will forever enslave himself to his typical negative reaction to any conflict. He is working on the premise of *"It's your fault."*

Suppose a third party in the room, let's call him Joe, became involved because Andy asked him for his opinion. Andy said, "Excuse me, Joe, I know that you just witnessed what happened between Reggie and me. I'm sure I was probably unaware of some of the areas of disagreement. Would you help by giving me your opinion on how

I could have responded differently to the situation to come to some type of amiable agreement?"

Immediately, Joe becomes engaged and begins to explain his own observations.

"First of all, Andy, you might not have realized it, but immediately after Reggie entered the room your tone of voice and volume started to escalate. As I was watching, I could see that Reggie perceived that you were ready to fight, so he started out on the defensive.

"Secondly, your posture as you approached Reggie was confrontational. Your physical approach to him became somewhat threatening.

"Third, at one point in the conversation, Reggie tried to apologize to you, but you completely ignored him."

In those few brief moments, Joe was able to pin down some amazing observations that could give Andy a completely different viewpoint and allow him to respond in a way that would bring about a different outcome. But Andy needed to ask for his friend's input, and be open to it. Sometimes that is not easy for us to do.

OBJECTIVITY—BECOMING THE THIRD PARTY

You learn to develop a mature approach to disputes when you are able to step outside of yourself and become your own third party. You are able to look at the situation objectively to see what good could come out of it, if you can just keep your attitude right. Initially, this requires enough humility to allow yourself the freedom to examine your own personal shortcomings. From this humility, you are able to gain a new sense of objectivity.

When I was first starting out in business, I had a friend who faced a terrible bankruptcy. The financial loss and the emotion involved hit him hard. He began to suffer from depression, and he avoided thinking about and talking about the bankruptcy. He believed if he just pushed it out of his mind, he would be able to get over it faster. Ironically, his breakthrough didn't come until he began to revisit the events leading up to the bankruptcy and do some evaluation of the situation. This required him to take a mental and emotional step back to look at what happened from a different perspective.

By doing so, he was able to clearly see the variables that led to his bankruptcy. Some were a result of his personal mismanagement of his business, and he was able to, with humility, examine those shortcomings. But he was also able to clearly see the major influence of the economy of that time and how he was impacted by that major shift. With this newfound clarity, he was able to adapt and adjust his personal perspective and not fully take the blame for circumstances that were beyond his control. By stepping into the role of being his own third party, he was able to learn from his mistakes and to let go of the deep emotional strain he had put himself under. His internal conversation shifted and became more constructive so that the bankruptcy, as painful as it was, became a learning experience.

Adversity will come in each of our lives at one time or another to varying degrees. Obstacles that seem insurmountable will block your way. By programming yourself to see them as challenges and stepping-stones to success, you will be able to free yourself from the swamp of disillusion and depression.

It is your task and responsibility to be rigorous in your effort to control the most important conversation of your life—the one you have with yourself.

3C EXERCISE

In the past, have you been able to love your life and learn from your setbacks?

- Often, remembering times where we felt overwhelmed but ended up in triumph is helpful and empowering. Has there been a personal story of recovery in your life or someone you know who continues to inspire you? What are the lessons that you can apply from this story?

- What have been you views on Recovery and Avoidance?

- What has been your experience with the most important conversation of your life—the one you have with yourself? Has it been empowering? How can you change to make improvements?

- Consider a time in your past of a specific setback. After having gained time and perspective, how can you see the situation differently? As you consider this situation, how did your perspective change and what did you learn that you can apply to similar obstacles in the future?

- Consider your life as a timeline that maps out the high and low points but has a continuing upward moving trend. Think of ways you can use this perspective when you are met with short-term challenges and obstacles.

Use these questions to help you gain your own third-party perspective and begin seeing your setbacks in a positive light. Use the *3C Companion Guide* to record your responses to these and further questions.

You're almost through to the end in completing this material. Keep reengaging in the practical sections using the 3C Exercises and the *3C Companion Guide* to make this investment of time something that will truly be impacting.

CHAPTER 11

3C VISUALIZATION

"I skate to where the puck is going
to be, not where it has been."
—WAYNE GRETZKY, retired as leading point
scorer in national hockey league history

POSITIVE MENTAL VISUALIZATION
BY OLYMPIC ATHLETES

All of us have started strong on some new diet, exercise routine, or project, or turned over a new leaf in the proverbial New Year's resolutions only to leave them behind a short while later. We have bought new treadmills, bikes, exercise equipment, that after a few months have become expensive coat racks pushed into the corner.

In my early years, I must admit that was my pattern. It was often difficult for me to stay focused on any new strategy. I found mental training makes the difference between success and failure, so we must learn to engage in this process. This essential key has been well documented in many areas.

In one of the most well-known studies on visualization, Russian scientists compared three groups of Olympic athletes, rating their physical and mental visualization ratios.

- *Group 1* received 100 percent physical training.

- *Group 2* received 75 percent physical training with 25 percent mental training.

- *Group 3* received 50 percent mental training with 50 percent physical training.

Remarkably, Group 3 had the best performance results. Similar studies validate that mental training has significant, measurable effects on lasting performance. Engaging active mental training, or in some of us retraining, involves the focused visualization and mental reinforcement of our intended goals.

Similarly, the past decade has seen a marked increase in the number of companies and executives who are hiring executive coaches.

However, these sessions may produce only *short-term gains*—a honeymoon effect—in many cases, unfortunately, the initial impact quickly wanes. At first, there seems to come a leveling up. Then there is a return to former levels or even lower.

To accomplish lasting change, the best executive coaching delivers permanent changes in deeper areas such as perceptions, lifestyles, and culture of the company.

I've come to believe that one of the most profound core skills necessary to uncap the hidden wealth within, to release the treasure and destiny of our lives, is to recognize and eliminate internal saboteurs that continually defeat us. There are many internal factors that cause us to give up before we start. Almost always they are rooted in our subconscious. Take the steps to become a champion over your thought life and you will be effective and prosperous on a consistent basis.

POSITIVE VISUALIZATION

Recently, I had to convene a fairly high-level national board of directors. Being a relational person, I enjoy connecting with people in a casual, relaxed environment. There are times when my business necessitates more formality, but convening a national board requires a high degree of formal proceedings. Feeling a little uneasy as the directors meeting approached, I took some time to practice positive visualization. In my mind's eye, I rehearsed the interactions and the meeting agenda, visualizing the best possible outcomes and positive responses I wanted to see happen. This produced a new level of confidence in me, and the board of directors meeting went even better than I had imagined.

As you practice positive visualization, start to visualize yourself in new settings related to your future prosperity. Then you can begin to get a picture of how your future self will look in order to be congruent with those surroundings. This small exercise can help you to see your future self in order to live in this new environment.

Visualize the person you want to be, what your relationships will look like, who you are, the types of endeavors you are embarking on, and how you are responding and interacting in these settings. Become rooted in "why" this new life is important. Mentally envision the related benefits of this new life and how this will help others around you.

Someone once profoundly stated, "No matter where you go, there you are." If we continually find ourselves in turmoil and friction among differing groups and environments, we

Each of us has the ability and the responsibility to change ourselves.

ourselves can be the common denominator. At a deeper level, each of us has the ability and the responsibility to change ourselves. Often in doing this internally, our external environment responds.

MENTAL DIET

For years, psychologists have tried to analyze where thoughts come from—what is their inception. The old adage "you are what you eat" cannot be more true when it comes to our mental diet. Therefore, you need to redirect your thought life to something significantly positive. When you focus on fulfilling a personal life plan that is supported by your own belief in that life plan, then your mind will stay occupied and progress is assured.

When you talk with people who are not deliberate about fulfilling their destiny, they may be passionate about generic goals. "I want to make money. I want to do this and that and make things happen."

However, when you ask, "What is your *personal* plan? Where are *you* going? What are *you* doing to fulfill *your* destiny?" they don't have a plan. And because they don't, they can't visualize their future clearly.

Initially, developing a life plan and creatively visualizing it may seem somewhat ethereal or hard to grasp. As you begin this process, it will become more clear, like focusing a camera lens.

PARTIAL SUCCESS

If you have been following along in the *3C Companion Guide,* I'm sure you're starting to see many of the elements of a plan for an effective, fulfilling life coming together. If you haven't been using the guide, I'm still confident that much of the material has helped clarify your course and identify some steps to a new path. In either case, keep in mind no one keeps to their plan 100 percent of the time, but even if you do it just 80 percent of the time, you will see results. Some days I wake up and I have a plan and I know what I am supposed to do. But I throw my plan aside and I say, "I'm going to go have coffee today." Doing that every now and then might not be too detrimental. I guarantee you that following a plan 80 percent of the time is a lot better than reaching 100 percent of no plan at all. A slip here and there does not mean you are failing. If you keep your life plan a large majority of the time, you are really clocking in with an A-level accomplishment.

SELF-PREOCCUPATION

I want to say at the outset of this process that I'm not a fan of continuous psychological self-evaluation. Internal psychological analysis is not what I'm advocating. This can lead to what I have called "Self-Preoccupation" where too much time is spent in self-focus and analysis. It has been my experience that prolonged self-analysis and other forms of critical introspection not only fails to produce the type of change we would like to see, but can lead us into a swamp, a downward spiral of psychological introspection. If you continually look for flaws in yourself, your past, or others, you're sure to find them.

A proactive, positive self-evaluation will draw out from you the type of person that you should be visualizing. This method of self-evaluation is geared to unearth those thoughts that are congruent with your own unique life direction and core purposes.

Your goal is not to discover how you have missed the mark or continually dredge up past pain. You seek to discover those characteristics to develop in your personality to prepare for the future, those internal treasures that make you unique among all people.

Once you define through self-discovery who you are and where you are going, you can build upon that strong foundation structures that will last.

PROACTIVE EVALUATION

Let's look at this from another standpoint. If you live a life that is not proactive, without positive visualization, then you are living

If you never take the time to visualize the life that you want to obtain, then you cannot reach the congruency between that picture and the process of maturity to make that picture a reality.

in a constant reactive state. This life is not based on igniting your passion, charting your course, or owning your life, but instead it's based on responding to other people's demands and expectations and the busyness and distraction of life. If you never take that time to clearly visualize the future prosperity and life that you want to obtain, then you cannot reach the congruency needed between that picture and the process of maturity in order to make that picture a reality. Make the choice today.

SETTING GOALS BASED ON
YOUR 3C STRATEGY

No matter how hard you try or how great your attitude, you will never get anywhere using the wrong map. Life goals are unique to each person, and though there may be some similarities, you cannot follow another person's plan as if their life map is identical to yours. If you try to apply the methods, systems, and tactics someone else has used to reach their personal goals and destinations in life, you will be disappointed. Your life is just too unique and personalized to do this.

UNIQUE GOALS

The diet guru, the self-help coach, and the business mogul who offers concrete steps to success in their realm of influence are vastly different from you. They have different body types, different upbringings, metabolisms, educations, and resources. In fact, the differences are infinite. They can be well-meaning and successful in their own individualized journey, but you can actually find yourself using the wrong map by trying to mimic them.

Whether in the realm of diet, finance, business development, or personal actualization, it is vital to understand that you cannot simply mimic the systems and methods of others. You must develop those that are unique and take into consideration your unique state.

Instead of looking for a detailed life plan from someone else, do the work yourself. Make it your ambition to gain understanding of the principles and thought-processes that go into living a fulfilling prosperous and high-impact life. Once you understand the methods and principles, you can apply them to your personal life plan and make your goals unique to your own lifestyle, personality, and starting point.

God took billions of atoms to form you as a distinct person. You have unique characteristics, passions, goals, and vision that have a distinctive place in this world. You were specifically designed like a key to fit a single lock. How many times have we fumbled through a key ring to find the right fit, none of the keys are bad, they just fit unique and specific locks.

PERSONAL VISION COLLECTION

Over the years year as I have found materials that inspired me, I have gathered them into a collection that I keep on hand.

In my personal collection, I have pages of inspirational quotes from great men and women that provide continuous encouragement for me. I have many personal development and executive self-assessment profiles. I also have pictures of orphanages and daycare centers I helped develop, so I can see the reality of the goals I have attained. There are also several personal notes from friends and loved ones and intimate goals I have yet to accomplish. This has helped me actualize my personal life convergence.

Life is a collision of unique gifts, passions, desires, and experiences that culminate in something that many have labeled convergence. Convergence is the point at which you are catapulted into your most important efforts. It is the amalgam of your unique self, gifting, training, and experiences. This combination creates a platform for our most rewarding and important accomplishments.

WHY SOME VISIONS FAIL

However, if you are like me, there have been times when you worked long and hard to obtain a goal—physical, financial, or social—and finally achieved your long sought-after objective only to find that it was anti-climactic. What went wrong?

I once worked very hard to be appointed to the board of directors for a very prestigious international organization. I had to send a curriculum vitae and recent news articles showing my accomplishments. I had to spend time "politicking" with current influential directors who could help approve my nomination. The whole process took more than a year.

Finally, I achieved my objective and was appointed in early January at the organization's annual meeting. For a while it was exciting. My name and picture went out through the newspapers. There was a host of new, influential people to meet. I was excited to take my wife to the annual Board Meeting Gala.

However, not long afterward, the excitement of my new appointment wore off, and we began the true business of the corporation. I found the meetings themselves to be dull and tedious. I found I had little in common with the other directors. I also realized I had not thoroughly recognized that my purpose as a director included fundraising. The other directors and I spearheaded several fundraising efforts that took considerable time and energy and required me to expend a lot of social capital as I called on associates to make financial commitments.

After serving one complete two-year term, I decided not to seek reappointment. This caused other directors to feel slightly uneasy about me. I told them I had conflicting time commitments and other obligations, but it somehow didn't fit with the zeal and eagerness of my initial appointment.

I didn't search my true intentions to see if my objective was congruent with my life as a whole. I was focused so heavily on my initial task that I had not pictured my goal, once achieved, as a lasting lifestyle commitment.

3C EXERCISE

The *3C Companion Guide* (available for free at www.DaveYarnes. com) has expanded material for this and other sections designed to give you space to develop a 3C Plan.

Now that your personal plan has grown using the 3C Exercises, take time to review the answers to previous 3C Exercises. Consolidate and rewrite your material from the question and the *3C Companion Guide* into a format that is easy to reference. Start preparing this material to be available and easily referenced on a weekly basis.

- What defines your own personal fulfilment and prosperity?

- What important roles and relationships in your life create true fulfilment?

- Take the time to envision yourself in these situations as though you were living in the future already. What character traits will you have to grow?

- What sort of nature and skill set will you have to have to live congruently with this new future self?

CHAPTER 12

PARTING THOUGHTS— GETTING READY FOR THE REST OF YOUR LIFE

"If you can't fly then run, if you can't run then walk, if you can't walk then crawl, but whatever you do, you have to keep moving forward."

—MARTIN LUTHER KING, JR.

THE NEXT STEP

Your next step could possibly be one of the most important in your life. Henry Ford once said, "Whether you think you can, or you think you can't—you're right." What do you think is the critical next step toward charting your course? Decide right now to be proactive. A lot of it comes down to how much you really want to change and become the person that you were intended to be. This comes from fully engaging in the process to transform the three circles of Spirit, Skill, and Self-Mastery.

It's important to strongly begin new lifestyle changes, so those routines that you want to change can take a strong root right from the beginning. It's important to take stock and identify those areas of your 3C Strategy that you wish to have the most significant growth. Self-discipline can be the deciding factor between achieving deep, substantial change or momentary superficial reorientation.

Please check your bookstore or e-vendor for my other resources. I hope you find enriching material. If you have any questions or comments, let me know at Info@DaveYarnes.com. Please take a look at www.DaveYarnes.com for further resources and information about our live events. You can also make an event request at Info@Daveyarnes.com.

If you haven't been using the *3C Companion Guide*, decide right now to download it at www.DaveYarnes.com—it's free. If you have been challenged and feel inspired to take the next steps to ignite your passion, chart your course, and own your fulfilling and prosperous life, the free *3C Companion Guide* can help you and track each area of your personal 3C Strategy. It contains additional exercises and resources designed to help. It also provides a format to develop your 3C life plan. You should reference this and review it often. This will help you stay on track and keep encouraged by noting your progress.

Regardless of how much you feel you lack or how much you feel you've already gained, I assure you that taking the time and working through the accompanying *3C Companion Guide* will make a significant impact.

You'll find some areas of your personal 3C Strategy are relatively easy to change. For other areas, the desire to succeed can be a determining factor. Face any self-defeating mindsets head-on. Even if you are moving into uncharted territory where you are sensing some anxiety or possibly fear, remember that even the most significant people often "do it afraid"—it's not the absence of apprehension, but it's the perseverance and the action to move forward, even with the existence of fear, anxiety, and doubt around us that makes the difference.

Make your priority those key elements that can bring about lasting, significant, and fulfilling change in your life. Avoid being at the mercy of other people's urgent requests. Think again about what priorities and principles are really substantial to you, and decide to engage in those things that are truly important. Just because something isn't urgent or screaming at you with a deadline, doesn't mean that it isn't one of the most important things in your life.

The Three Circle Strategy becomes the operating system for many plans in life. Whether you are wanting to focus on dieting, exercise, weight loss, entrepreneurial ventures, advancing in your company, strengthening your marriage, or growing your family, all of them require a plan, focus, skill, passion, and divine help or direction.

To drive this information deeper, buy this book for someone else as a gift and encourage them in the application of the material. This is not a veiled attempt at selling more books, I have honestly learned that trying to teach and convey material to others drives the information and meaning into a deeper level. I have tried my best to make the content, size, and price conducive to this being the kind of gift I personally would like to give or receive.

I also highly recommend attending one of our live events. These focus on: The Three Circle Strategy for a Fulfilling Life, Time Management, Fulfilling your Destiny, and other important topics. These are held in various locations or on an individual basis to an organization, you can find out more about how to participate at www.DaveYarnes.com. The ability for you to be in a "live environment," to ask questions and get individual feedback as you ignite your passion, chart your course, and own your life is incomparable. The interaction "band width" and interchange is invigorating at these live events.

Make the choice to create a lifestyle that continually strives for the fulfilling, prosperous life you were designed to enjoy.

When you face setbacks, remember that they are common parts of all of our lives. Make the choice to create a lifestyle that continually strives for the fulfilling, prosperous life you were designed to enjoy. Life can get busy and be filled with distractions.

Without intentionality, the less important aspects (the cares, concerns, errands, and worries) can crowd out our focus on those things that truly matter.

It all comes down to choices, self-discipline, and self-control. As you move forward from here, make a commitment to yourself to never let those things that truly matter be at the mercy of those that don't. Ignite your passion, chart your course, and own your life. More fulfilment and accomplishment than you have ever imagined begins now.

 3C EXERCISE

Getting Ready for the Rest of Your Life

- What actions can you take to strongly begin new life-style changes?

- How can you take your answers, reflections, and directions from all of the 3C Exercises and *3C Companion Guide* and keep them in front of you on a daily basis?

- Which routines can you change to allow your 3C Strategy to grow strong roots right from the beginning?

- Self-discipline can be the deciding factor between achieving deep, substantial change or superficial reorientation. How can you grow in this area?

The *3C Companion Guide* (available for free at www.DaveYarnes. com) can be saved as a type of life journal once completed. Consider purchasing a journal or a notebook for this reason. You can print and store your *3C Companion Guide* and the responses to the 3C Exercises in one place. I use mine to include personality profiles, inspirational writings, and many things that keep me inspired and directed. Putting all of these items in one place is designed to give you space to reflect and comment and has a format that can be stored and referenced. You can often refer back to track your progress and adjust your answers as your growth in the Three Circles continues for a lifetime. Be sure to write us at Info@DaveYarnes.com to share your breakthroughs. We enjoy reading your comments and feedback and helping with any questions.

My deepest and most sincere desire, as well as my heartfelt prayer, is that as you read and apply this material you ignite your passion, chart your course, and own your life in your fulfilling and prosperous future.

ABOUT DR. DAVE YARNES

Dr. Dave Yarnes represents a unique voice in business today. He has been a serial entrepreneur for the last 30 years. He is in high demand as an executive coach, consultant, and keynote speaker. Dave's humor, candor, and spiritual insight paints a picture of business and personal development that is not often seen.

You can contact Dave at www.DaveYarnes.com